# The Power of Giving and Gratitude!

*A Path to Creating Your Reality*

D1384093

by
Anthony DeNino

Library of Congress Cataloging-in-Publication Data

DeNino, Anthony – 1967 -
*The Power of Giving and Gratitude* by Anthony DeNino

This book will expand your mind and lay out plans that will help you live a more meaningful, powerful, and impactful life.

1. Kindness   2. Reality   3. Giving 4. Metaphysical
I. DeNino, Anthony, 1967 - II. Metaphysical  III. Kindness   IV. Title

Library of Congress Catalog Card Number: 2019949816
ISBN: 9781940265681


Cover Art and Layout: Victoria Cooper Art
Book set in: Sitka, Times New Roman
Book Design: Tab Pillar
Published by:

PO Box 754, Huntsville, AR 72740
800-935-0045 or 479-738-2348; fax 479-738-2448
WWW.OZARKMT.COM


Printed in the United States of America

# Dedication

We all have that one person in life that we come to realize means everything to us. That extension of who you are, who knows your thoughts, your beliefs, your dreams, your nightmares, your failures, and your triumphs. For me it is the true love of my life, my wife, Dianne. From the moment we fell in love, she has been my rock and to this day remains "my inspiration." Thank you, baby, for your support all these years, for your encouraging words, and for your incredible help as my first editor in making this book become a reality. My love for you grows exponentially by the day.

In addition to all that she is above, Dianne is also the mother of our beautiful girls, Meaghan and Sarah. To my girls—whom I am so proud of in every way—please consider what is written in this book because, in part, it was written for you to help in both the victorious and the difficult times that life brings.

I love my three ladies with all that I am.

# Table of Contents

# Prologue

We are at a tipping point!

Review any Internet news feed, watch any local or cable news station, or pick up any newspaper and what will it be filled with? Stories about negative, energy-draining events that have taken place in your own neighborhood, if not your city, state, and around the world. Talk about depressing!

And while they may not all be life-and-death stories, they are the type of stories that can have a disturbing impact on your life and the way you see it when you consistently and repeatedly hear about them.

**That stops here!**

Like other problems, there is a solution. The solution you'll read about in this book focuses on tools each and every one of us has at hand. At any moment you need them, they are there. They are at your beck and call and to varying degrees, you are more than likely using them already.

It doesn't matter if you're rich or poor. The color of your skin is irrelevant. It makes no difference what nationality you represent. Tall or short. Skinny or heavy. You may have received your education from the finest institution in the world or you may not have made it out of the seventh grade. Whoever you are, whatever your background, whatever you do or want to accomplish in life, this book will positively impact you beyond your expectations.

What you are about to read is steeped in proof, both medical and scientific. It will call on your spiritual beliefs that will all intersect with real-life stories about everyday people and some of the more famous people throughout history.

Welcome to *The Power of Giving and Gratitude!*

In addition to what is referenced above, this book will expand your mind and lay out plans that will help you to live a more meaningful, more powerful, and more impactful life. In the process of living this enhanced life, you will also help others do the same.

This book promises to help you have a closer relationship with your body, your mind, and your soul while bringing into your life a more meaningful relationship with God.

You've heard the old proverb, "It takes a village … ," right? Well, I'm happy to let you know that all it takes to have a lasting impact on the world is one person. You!

# Chapter One
# The Meaning of Life (Part I)

**Vision Statement of CORe—Creating Our Reality, Inc.**
*To live in a world where a person's success is truly measured by the
number of other people one helps to achieve their goals in life.*

Well, as you can see from the title of this chapter, I like to tackle big
topics. So, let's get right to it.

What is the meaning of life? This is a question that has been
debated by philosophers, scientists, religious scholars, and people at
your neighborhood bar for centuries. Answers vary and can range
from understanding all that life has to offer, living our lives as Jesus
or Buddha did, or by making the most of our abilities. And these are,
like most others, great answers.

After fifty-plus years of living and observing this beautiful
thing we call life, however, I'd like to explain to you what I have
discovered and how it ties in all of the above responses you may
believe or have heard throughout your life. The meaning of life
centers around your abilities—and every single person out there has
these abilities—to give to others and to be thankful for all you have
in your life.

Simply put, the meaning of life is giving and gratitude.

It is about the joy others experience and about your own joy
when giving to someone else. It is about the deep-rooted sincerity
of being thankful and appreciative for the things you *do* have in life

and not frustrated or disappointed by what you don't.

The effects of giving and gratitude, as you are about to learn, are measurable. They are measurable in terms of your physical, mental, and emotional health and well-being ... not to mention the positive impact they have on others.

How one gives to others can be achieved through a myriad of avenues. Being thankful and showing gratitude, likewise. For now, though, let's touch on giving.

You see it everywhere you look. People showing and exhibiting kind acts to other people—strangers in some cases. But here's the question: Do you allow yourself to acknowledge it?

By showing kindness, you are giving to other people, even if it is something simple like waiting those extra two seconds—though it seems like two minutes—to hold a door open for somebody.

You know what I'm talking about. You're walking into a convenience store and out of the corner of your eye you see somebody coming up behind you. They're at that "tipping point" of sorts, though, so you ask yourself, *"Can I go in without holding the door open but not looking like a jerk?"* Or, is it too close to call so you tell yourself, *"I'll be nice and wait?"* It's a mental conundrum I've often battled.

Or perhaps it's something more involved; for example, taking time out of your day to spend it with a friend who's going through a tough time. *"I mean c'mon, it's Saturday. I've busted my butt all week and I need some 'me' time,"* you reason. *"But,"* the inner dialogue continues, *"I really have the opportunity to help my buddy who's always been there for me."*

Giving your attention, your energy, and your efforts to another person is a far more profound way of giving than, say, by giving money. That is not to say that giving money isn't important, because it's often utilized as a wonderful and important way to help others, including yourself, as you'll shortly read about.

But back to my question. Do you allow yourself to acknowledge it? I'm going to go out on a limb here and make the statement that most people don't recognize the kindness that is all around them. Now I'm not suggesting that we go out and build a shrine to every person who says or does something kind for another; however, think about yourself for a moment. I mean, there is some level of satisfaction you feel when you help somebody, right?

Surely you give yourself that silent "pat on the back" for being nice. After all, you've made a difference in their day in ways that may be evident, but also in ways that may not be. It could even be something as simple as giving a hug.

Do you know who Juan Mann is? Have you heard of the Free Hugs campaign? Juan Mann is the person who started this movement in 2004. His story goes like this:

> I'd been living in London when my world turned upside down and I'd had to come home. By the time my plane landed back in Sydney, all I had left was a carry-on bag full of clothes and a world of troubles. No one to welcome me back, no place to call home. I was a tourist in my hometown.
>
> Standing there in the arrivals terminal, watching other passengers meeting their waiting friends and family, with open arms and smiling faces, hugging and laughing together, I wanted someone out there to be waiting for me. To be happy to see me. To smile at me. To hug me.
>
> So I got some cardboard and a marker and made a sign. I found the busiest pedestrian intersection in the city and held that sign aloft, with the words "Free Hugs" on both sides.[1]

He concludes his story, saying,

> And for 15 minutes, people just stared right through me. The first person who stopped, tapped me on the shoulder and told me how her dog had just died that morning. How that morning had been the one-year anniversary of her only daughter dying in a car accident. How what she needed now, when she felt most alone in the world, was a hug. I got down on one knee, we put our arms around each other and when we parted, she was smiling.
>
> Everyone has problems and for sure mine haven't compared. But to see someone who was once frowning, smile even for a moment, is worth it every time.[2]

---

1    https://www.freehugscampaign.org/.
2    https://www.freehugscampaign.org/.

Let's look at this a little more closely.

One man, committing the one small act of giving out hugs, positively impacted total strangers through the smiles and appreciation he gave. And do you think he also got something out of all those hugs? You bet.

And here's the really cool thing. Other people, in other countries, started replicating his Free Hugs campaign with equal success.

Do you think there's a simple act of giving you can do that will result in having a worldwide effect? Perhaps there is but even if it doesn't have that wide-reaching effect, focus on the one or two people it does impact because it truly means the world to them.

The next time you do something nice for somebody, whether it is something simple or something that has you going out of your way, be on notice. On notice for their reaction. On notice for their sincerity. On notice for their gratitude. You'll often find that they smile, look you in the eye, and express a really sincere thank-you.

But that is not everybody. Some people take it further as exhibited by Matt Ryan of Clifton Park, New York, who was at a Brugger's Bagel Bakery in Delmar, New York, one day. Here is the story Matt tells:

> What a crazy morning. To start, I left my wallet at home and I needed it to pay for parking. My wonderful wife, Keri, was kind enough to bring it to me in the pouring rain. So now, we are both soaked. Just as I was thinking, "What a great morning I was having," a very kind woman decided to pay for my breakfast. I was blown away! I then decided to keep it going and pay for the person behind me. This woman's actions continued for at least the next 7 customers! So, at a time when all the news is either political and/or negative, it is nice to see someone take action to make someone else's day positive. Thank you to this kind stranger for helping to make my day positive!!

This is an amazing story because not only does it talk about giving … by the acts of Matt's wife and the woman who bought his breakfast … but by the gratitude and actions he and the (at least) seven other customers also exemplified.

To be clear, however, this story is not how it always happens.

How many of you have shown kindness to a stranger, gone out of your way for a friend, or gave up your time and energy to help a loved one only to get nothing in return? Not even a simple thank-you, let alone any sincerity. A smile for your efforts? Uh-Uh! And then you get upset, angry, and maybe even say to the person in a frustrated tone, "You know, you could've at least said thanks!"

I know I have and still sometimes fall into that thought process. I mean, it's just common courtesy, isn't it?

Here's my question, though, and it may hurt a bit because I know it hurt me: Why did you **really** help that person out?

Did you do it for the accolades? For the gratitude? So you could tell others what a great person you are? Or, did you wonder since you're helping another out, what will he/she do in return for you? Too many people get caught up in what we are getting in return versus just focusing on helping somebody out … just for the sake of giving, of being kind, and for making a difference in the life of another human being.

Let me tell you about my younger self.

I have always considered myself a giving person but noticed at this particular time in my life, the nicer things I was doing weren't being reciprocated in any way. It started getting me really upset.

Are you familiar with the term "quid pro quo?" If not, it simply means doing something for somebody in return for that person doing something for you.

As a result of getting nothing in return, I began thinking about *Silence of the Lambs* when Anthony Hopkins's and Jodie Foster's characters were talking about "quid pro quo." It was the part of the movie when Dr. Lechter would give information to Clarise to help her solve a crime, only to have Clarise share personal information about herself.

At this point in my life, I'd find myself thinking, *"C'mon, man, quid pro quo! Where's my quid pro quo?!"* Do you remember the song by Dire Straits titled "Money for Nothing?" In that song, they sing, *"I want my, I want my, I want my MTV ..."* Well, for me, it became, *"I want my, I want my, I want my quid pro quo."*

But of course, it never came.

It really bothered me but when I had that little heart-to-heart with myself and started looking at the bigger picture, I began to realize that other people's actions—*or lack thereof*—should play no role in the way I act. If I was going to help somebody out, then I was going to help somebody out. No strings attached. Just me trying to be a good person and being kind, for the sake of being a good person and being kind. No strings attached!

*"But that's not the world we live in,"* may be your reply. *"More than ever, people today are all about themselves and they're not changing,"* you may continue in an effort to give your point of view more validity.

My response is simple.

It may not be the world we live in now (though I believe that would be an incorrect statement), but here's the beautiful thing if this is your belief: **Y-O-U** have the power and ability to change it, beginning in this very moment to change the world, to change how you view others, and to change your reality. Now this is a huge undertaking, trying to change the entire world, so instead, let's work on changing *your* world. Let's work on making those small, seemingly insignificant changes that can make all the difference.

Changing your world reminds me of one of my favorite quotes by the recently anointed Saint Teresa. Now keep in mind, I'm talking about Saint Teresa, whom you may better know as Mother Teresa, with her beautiful thoughts, beliefs, and actions. She was a woman who quite literally could've changed the world all by herself. But even she said this:

I alone cannot change the world, but I can cast a stone across the waters to create many ripples.

My translation is that she knew she couldn't change every single person all on her own. As much as she was this worldwide figure of goodness, love, and compassion, this was just too much for one person to accomplish. However, if she and other people worked on changing *their* world, then little by little, house by house, town by town, city by city, state by state, and country by country, the world could indeed change. And change for the better!

We can all point to instances in our lives where somebody was rude or ungrateful for something ... and maybe it even happened earlier today ... however, it is now all about going forward and making lasting, positive changes that will affect generations!

**You** have this power! **You** have this ability! It is a matter of believing in the impact that you, this one little person, in this big, giant world we live in, can have on so many others. It is not a process that happens overnight but do you know what? The attitudes and actions of people today didn't happen overnight either. And regarding the "that's not the world we live in" comment, I ask you this, "Who do you think created this world?" People! Me, you, your family, my neighbors and friends. People from all walks of life, from tiny towns to major cities. From small, third-world countries to the world's superpowers.

Sure, we can take the easy way out and blame things like the press, greed, and social media but guess who's at the forefront of all those things? People!

The first step is to acknowledge this. It's about taking responsibility and owning up to the role we've all played in the actions that are taken today. I don't point that out in an effort to collectively kick us while we're down, but rather as a way to recognize the problem and go forward from this point on. There is absolutely nothing we can do about the past; we can only go forward and live in this moment.

But now the beautiful thing, and it's simply this. Just as we've created the negative events and attitudes, we can also create the positive version of those things. It is entirely up to us as individuals, and all it takes is one brave person to step out and be the guiding light in their world. Not as if you are some kind of savior, but rather, as a person who becomes the living embodiment of kindness. Of giving and of gratitude.

You have it in you. Everybody has it in them. It is a matter of bringing it out. Now granted, this is a task that is easier to accomplish on some versus others, but it is inside each and every one of us … with NO exceptions.

Boy or girl. Man or woman. Whether you're a CEO or somebody just starting their career. Young or old. Gainfully employed or unemployed. Whatever your situation may be, whoever you are, wherever you are in life, you have it in you!

Let me offer these suggestions to get the ball rolling. Be nice. Be kind. Be polite. Be friendly. And when you see somebody walking down the street—whether you know them or not—smile. The art of a simple and sincere smile can go a long way, as we'll find out later in chapter 7.

Do you know somebody—a family member, friend, or co-worker—who walks around in what seems like a perpetual bad mood? He/she always sees the negative and is suspicious of everybody they come across. It's the one who always seems to have that dark, menacing cloud over their head that follows them wherever they go and is the type who always asks themselves in a sinister-sounding voice, "What does this person *really* want from me?"

If you are a Law of Attraction person like I am—or even if you're not—you most likely understand that "like attracts like," meaning that if you are always expecting something bad or negative to happen, and just "knowing" you'll see the worst in people, then chances are you won't be disappointed.

Well, it works both ways.

If you walk around intent on being nice, kind, polite, friendly, and always ready to smile at somebody, then guess what? You'll get more of that in return than you ever have before. You'll notice a warmth and sincerity coming back from others, and it's all because you decided you wanted to give to that person.

And let's be clear, this is a form of giving. Here, you are giving of yourself. Something that is inside you and something you are making an effort to share with the world. And that, my friends, is a beautiful thing.

Still not convinced?

Then try this.

In different parts of this book, I am going to ask you to accomplish some things. But first, let me ask you a question. When faced with tasks or that seemingly never-going-to-end number of things that you have to get done, do you make out a list? A lot of people refer to this as a "Things To Do" list or TTD. I was a notorious TTD list maker.

But no more. I still make lists, but now it's a little different. I refer to it as a "TTA" or *"Things To Accomplish"* list. The reason for this is because nobody likes to have to "do" things. They are chores. They're jobs. It's work. Everybody, however, likes to feel "accomplished." Everybody enjoys the end result of completing a project. Everybody likes the feeling of putting that check mark by their list and scratching off the item. Instead of "doing" it, though, accomplish it! Plus, it just sounds cooler.

For your first TTA—and I've included a layout at the end of this chapter that you may choose to follow—I am asking for your *"Commitment of Three."* For the next three days, I am asking for your dedication and sincere efforts in giving in one of the following ways: your time, your kindness, your money, your attention, your sincerity, your love, your respect, your admiration, your effort, your friendship.

And here is all you need to do.

From the ten options I gave you (or feel free to add your own form of giving), choose three of them and fully commit for the next three days to make them a part of your life. They could be implemented with family, friends, co-workers, strangers, and even nature, but focus on, for example, giving your time, showing kindness, and showing your admiration to those in your world. You can accomplish this through whatever means you see fit; however, here are some ideas: Do you have a parent(s) living on their own? Perhaps there's an opportunity to take an hour out of your day and talk with them. Reminisce about some of the good times you've had, maybe cut their lawn for no reason, or clean out the garage and let them know how much you admire all that they've accomplished in life … even if you think the only great thing they accomplished was having a wonderful kid like you.

The key to your actions having the desired impact will be your sincerity in doing them, and by your expectations. In other words, by expecting nothing in return.

Then, take time. Time to notice. Notice the warmth in people's eyes, the appreciation, and overall reaction to your giving. In all honesty, however, you may experience some cynicism along the way and people wondering what your "angle" is. But don't let them distract you. They're obviously not ready to receive your kindness or giving ways. That's unfortunate but if you run into these people, just wish them a good day and move on to your next act.

Then finally, and perhaps most important, notice you. Notice how you felt during your actions, how you felt following your encounters, and how you've started wondering how you can keep this going after your three days are up. **HINT:** You can do it for the rest of the week. You can do it for the rest of the month. Heck, the real goal here is for you to get so comfortable and confident in living in this manner that you can keep going for the rest of your life and notice an even greater impact on yourself and others!

Changing the world, or even your world, is not easy because it takes a consistent, concerted effort to make this happen. However, it is not as difficult as you may have previously thought. The key is to not wait for others to take action. Even if you are the type of person who doesn't like attention or taking the lead on things, this is something that can be done in a very low-key, nonchalant manner, yet, still have the tremendously positive impact we desire.

And if you are looking to do this activity with others, fantastic! Ask your family, friends, and/or co-workers to conduct their own experiments based on the above criteria. Teachers, this would be a great activity for your class. Think about the impact this will have on your students and school. Managers/executives, this would be a great morale booster and employee bonding experience.

Parents? What a great lesson to teach your kids while they are still young and not so jaded by some of the attitudes that are given attention in society today. This would be a great way to show them how good life—and other people—can really be.

Don't be shy about the results. A great way to help an endeavor like this expand is by letting others know all about it, so please send me an e-mail and let me know how it went. My contact information is at the back of the book.

*** 

Earlier I touched on how money is a great and much-needed way to give. But here's a really amazing fact. When it comes to having more money versus giving money to help others, people are happier when they actually give it than receive it. There is undoubtedly a short-term high when you receive more money—for example, a raise at work—being able to purchase something of a material manner; however, unless you are being brought out of poverty, people are far and away happier by spending money on others.

In fact, the authors of a study reviewed in the April 17, 2008, edition of the *Harvard Gazette* for the article titled "Money Spent on Others Can Buy Happiness" by Colleen Walsh, the following was stated:

*Michael Norton, assistant professor of business administration in the marketing unit at the Harvard Business School (HBS), conducted a series of studies with his colleagues Elizabeth Dunn and Lara Aknin at the University of British Columbia (UBC). Together they showed that people are happier when they spend money on others versus on themselves. The results were published last month in the journal, Science.*

"This study addressed a paradox that economists have talked about for a long time—that increases in income don't tend to lead to big increases in happiness," said Norton. "People buy bigger and bigger houses, but they don't seem to get much happier as a result."

In fact, "The findings showed that those who reported spending more on others, what the team called 'prosocial' spending, also reported a greater level of happiness, while how much they spent on themselves had no impact on happiness."

A few years ago, I had the opportunity to witness something beautiful. I was waiting to check out in a grocery store and was a few customers separated from the front of the line. I noticed, though, that a woman was having issues with her debit or credit card. The issues weren't due to a fading of the black strip on the back or because it wasn't fitting into the slot properly. The issue was that there wasn't enough money available to pay for her groceries.

When something like this happens, I feel it would be a very interesting social experiment because there are some people who get angry because they have to wait in line a little longer, others pretend they don't notice what's happening, some will just observe, and then there is the last kind of person. This person is the coolest person in the room because without judging, he's the one who is willing to help.

I observed the man explain to the woman that I'm sure there is a problem with the card itself but in the meantime, he said, let me pay for your groceries. After some initial resistance, she relented. She was incredibly grateful, a little embarrassed, but mostly relieved as she smiled a huge smile walking out.

Witnessing something like this is inspiring. It is a regeneration of the human spirit that reminds us of the kindness and giving attitude that we all possess. It was so inspiring, in fact, that a few months later, I was the guy directly behind a different woman in the store. Pretty much the same scenario played out with the only difference being that she was able to pay for some of her food.

As I was watching, I noticed the foods she put back were the type of foods you would make meals with—a roast, burgers, chicken—but she kept the mac and cheese and other nonessential foods. In other words, she purchased a larger number of the little foods and some kitchen supplies, but nothing of substance. She kept her head down throughout the process and walked out of the store.

I wanted to do something but at the time I knew at my home, there were some financial concerns as well. Quickly, however, I came to the realization that she needed help ... and that we'd find a way. At that point, I had the cashier ring up the foods the woman left behind and had a bagger run out and catch the woman in the parking lot before she left.

I was thinking based on her reaction in the store, a neutral party was better to bring her the foods than me so I just watched from a distance as she smiled, looked around in an effort to figure out who did this, and went on her way.

I tell these stories so as to point out just another way you can make a difference. I (and the other guy) am certainly not the first person to do something like this and won't be the last. However, to give, to help, and to bring joy to another person are precious times in life ... not to mention the incredible joy it brought to me.

In another experiment, "Researchers at UBC handed envelopes of money to students on campus. The recipients were told they should spend the money (either $5 or $20) by the end of that day either on themselves—to cover a bill or expense or get themselves a gift—or on others, a gift for someone or a donation to charity.

"The results mirrored those from their other studies," the article states. The experiment concludes, "We found that people who spent the money on themselves that day weren't happier that evening," said Norton, "but people who spent it on others were. The amount of money, $5 or $20, didn't matter at all. It was only how people spent it that made them happier."[3]

Five dollars. Twenty dollars. Whatever the amount of money may be (and we'll talk about "Proportionate Giving" in a later chapter) to not only help another person out, but also to help make

---

3 "Money Spent on Others Can Buy Happiness," *Harvard Gazette*, April 17, 2008. http://news.harvard.edu/gazette/story/2008/04/money-spent-on-others-can-buy-happiness.

you happier, is something we can all strive for and achieve.

Little by little, day by day, and small action by small action taken, will be the start of exponential growth, development, and happiness in the world. The really exciting part is that it all begins with you, so take action right away. Don't think about it. Don't weigh the pros and cons. Don't call your family and friends to solicit their opinions. Take action and take action now!

If you need some further inspiration, then consider David Hill of Brooklyn, New York. We've all set New Year's resolutions in the past, right? Well, David made one that set the resolution business on its ear.

In an article that appeared in *GQ* magazine's January 1, 2016, edition, David Hill's New Year's resolution from a couple of Decembers ago, was written about. It was, as he told the article's writer, Jonah Keri, the following:

> For the entire year to come, whenever anyone on the street asked him for money, he would give that person money. Every single time. No questions asked.
>
> "I mostly wanted to change my knee-jerk reaction from saying no all the time to saying yes all the time."

He had to set some rules, though.

> Rule number one: whenever he was asked for money, he would give the smallest denomination he had on him. If all he had was change, he would give all of his change— whether it was a nickel or more than a dollar's worth. If it was bills, he would hand over the smallest bill in his wallet. Often, it was a $1.00 bill. Other times it might be a five or ten.
>
> And sometimes it was a twenty.

Think about that for a moment. If he happened to stop and get cash out of an ATM that day, then guess what? They don't distribute singles and fives. Most distribute only $20.00 bills, though some give out $10.00 bills also. So, if he was caught at that right time, by that right person, he had no choice but to give him/her $20.00. The article continues, "Hill reckons he gave away twenties at least a half-dozen times that year."

Now if you find yourself thinking that $120.00 isn't that much money, I ask you to remember that David Hill lives in Brooklyn, New York, and if you haven't been there before, you may not know that there are far too many people, for various reasons, asking for money. As for David Hill, "he estimates the total damage for the year to be around $1,000.00."

But he didn't stop there.

Rule number two: treat someone asking for a specific thing—food, a swipe of your subway card—the same way you would someone who asks for money.

Rule number three: Be less suspicious. For years, whenever someone on a street corner asked for change, or a kid asked for money for basketball uniforms, Hill wondered if he was being conned. After a while, he started thinking, "who cares?" So if a man on the subway said he was a homeless veteran and needed a few bucks, Hill didn't think through whether he believed the guy—he would just reach into his pocket.

Finally, the article states, "He came to enjoy those ordinary encounters with ordinary New Yorkers—they became part of the reward."

The bottom line is this. We've all heard the expression "give until it hurts," right? Well, apparently, it should be "give until you're happy." Has a nice ring to it, don't you think?

In closing this chapter, let me say this. As was outlined, regardless of a person's financial status, there are so many ways we can make a positive difference in another's life. The question now becomes, will you, at the very least, take those extra two seconds or that $5.00 bill to potentially impact somebody else's day in a beneficial way?

# Things To Accomplish #1

## Commitment of Three—Day 1

### What & How I Gave Today

_____
_____
_____
_____

## Commitment of Three—Day 2

### What & How I Gave Today

_____
_____
_____
_____

## Commitment of Three—Day 3

### What & How I Gave Today

_____
_____
_____
_____

# Chapter Two
# The Meaning of Life (Part II)

**What is Gratitude?**

Dictionary.com defines gratitude as *the quality or feeling of being grateful or thankful*. Merriam Webster points to this definition: *a feeling of appreciation or thanks*. Well, I'm sure we all understand the "thanks" or "thankful" part but how much are we truly "feeling" when we say or give thanks?

Think about this. How many times do you hear somebody say, "Thank God?" This is a response I hear often—*even by people who don't believe in God*—and the thing that is curious to me is the tone of people's voices that are often used. Because here's the thing—we are speaking to the Almighty. The Creator. The one who has given us life. Yet most people when saying *"Thank God"* are using it with no tone, no thought, and no meaning. It's just something else to say.

What about this one: "How are you doing?" You know, you run into a friend or co-worker and say, "How are you doing?" Or if you're from New York as I am, it's more like, "Howyadoin'?" If you're from my adopted state of North Carolina, it's, "Heyyy" (we won't get into "Bless her heart"). It's the type of thing you say when you see somebody and it's an opening line. Most of the time people don't really care to know how the other person is doing, it's just something we say to others as a greeting. I'd estimate 95 percent of those say it without any emotion or meaning.

Regrettably, I admit, I still fall into that trap and am sometimes one of those 95 percenters.

To those who hear that question and feel (as you should) the person asking really does care about how you are doing, though, wow, you guys take it to heart. I have a friend who—*bless his heart*—I'll call and when I ask that question, he takes it to heart. I've figured him out, though. Before the call, I have to have a pep talk with myself because I KNOW I have to come with a certain agenda of things to accomplish on the call. I KNOW if I begin the conversation with, "Howyadoin'?" I won't get to speak for at least ten minutes ... and then I forget half of the things I wanted to talk about.

So when the big moment arrives and it's time to call, I go through this routine and psyche myself up by repeating my mantra, "Don't say howyadoin'! Don't say howyadoin'! Don't say howyadoin'!" He picks up and what do I say? "Hey, buddy. Howyadoin'?" I scream, "NOOOOOOOOOOOOOOO!!!" ... on the inside ... but it's too late. He goes on to tell me ALL the details of how he's doing.

To be clear, like most, it's not that I don't care but I sometimes fall into the trap of wanting to get things accomplished and getting them accomplished now. I sometimes don't feel that I have time for small talk. There are times when I don't want to take the time to learn every detail of what's going on in somebody else's life. I know that may sound harsh to some but I do believe in being truthful, which I feel is an important first step to changing behaviors.

Now, maybe we are sincere in saying "Thank God" and perhaps more than 5 percent of the population really does care about how *you* are doing. That being said, most times, there's no emotion. No sincerity. It's robotic in nature when most people say it. There is no *feeling* behind it.

And when there is no feeling behind what we say, is it genuine? When we express thanks to God, a family member, a friend, a co-worker, a stranger, or whomever without any emotion behind the sentiment, are we really showing gratitude? We are definitely saying the right thing, but again, are we feeling it?

And that's what I'd like to focus on for a bit, the feeling, and understanding the "why."

Dr. Laura Trice, a counselor, therapist, and life coach, conducted a very succinct (under four minutes), but no less impactful, TED talk titled "Remember to Say Thank You" and with some eloquence and humor, really nailed the importance of saying, "Thanks."

Among other points, she asks, "Why don't we tell people what we need?" and why the simple of act of giving a sincere and heartfelt "thank-you" makes a difference. To her, she goes on to point out: "I'm giving you critical data about me. I'm telling you where I'm insecure. I'm telling you where I need your help ..."

On a personal note, during those times when I expect to get something back when I give, that is, somebody taking the time to say and sincerely mean "thank you," I had never before considered the "why" behind my frustration when I don't hear it. Because of Dr. Trice's talk, however, I now understand why I feel this way when not receiving it. What she said really makes a lot of sense.

Last point on saying "thanks" or "thank you." As a society, as a race (human), it is my hope that we do things for others while expecting nothing in return. Just as I had discussed earlier, doing it for the sake of helping another out. With no expectation. That being said, when the recipient of the kind deed or action takes the time to offer a heartfelt thank-you, it really makes a difference.

I encourage you to view Dr. Trice's entire talk to better understand why this is so important. Check it out at https://www.ted.com/talks/laura_trice_suggests_we_all_say_thank_you?language=en.

As in giving, there are a number of ways one can show gratitude. You can be thankful in a verbal manner to an individual or group, with your body language, a sincere smile, or by paying it forward.

It is in another way, though, I'd like to focus on. And that is by being thankful to God, to have that dialogue, that conversation with Him in which you express your thanks.

For example, what kind of car do you drive? Is it the latest, top-of-the-line model that runs like a dream? Or, is it more the type that has you adding oil once a week, checking the coolant constantly, and saying far too often, "Hmmm, I've never heard *that* noise before?"

Now granted, we all would like to have the finer things in life. Realize, however, that if the car you are driving gets you from point A to B, then you are in better shape than a lot of others. It may not be the prettiest thing to look at, it may not purr like a kitten, but when you get frustrated about that, look around. Observe those people who have to wait at the bus stop, for example. Think about doing this in the sweltering heat, the bitter cold, or during a thunderstorm. Or worse yet, what about those who have to walk to work in these conditions?

If you allow yourself to get into that true feeling of gratitude, your older, beat-down, oil-leaking vehicle is now a thing of beauty. It is a blessing and something to be thankful for—*regardless of how it looks*—over and over again.

"OK, sure, but 'most everybody' drives to work," you may find yourself saying. "And when you take out major metropolitan cities like New York and Chicago, you really have everybody driving," you may add to give your argument even more validity.

Let's check these thoughts and put some real numbers to them. According to multiple sources, the population in the United States in March of 2017 alone is right at 326 million people. Of those, 196 million age sixteen and over are part of the workforce, according to the US Bureau of Labor Statistics. Overall, we are talking about roughly 60 percent of the population working.

Now, additional statistics put the number of those who drive to work at 76 percent, meaning that roughly 149 million people actually drive. And when you add another 10 percent to make the overall number of people who have access to a car (e.g., those who ride with another driver) as their means for getting to and from work, we are now at 168.6 million people.

Pretty strong numbers. However, as life is about perspective in my view, I ask you to consider this. Twenty-seven point four million people ... or written another way ... 27,400,000 people in the United States rely on public transportation or walking as the way they arrive at and leave from work—every single day—whether it's in the beautiful weather of San Diego or the rainy city of Seattle. During the brutally cold winters of Chicago or the desert-like temperatures of Phoenix, 27.4 million people in the US workforce do not have a vehicle of their own they can rely on for transportation.

The reason why I and so many others have vehicles whereas others don't, isn't clear. What should be clear, however, is that out of all the people in the country who don't have to battle the elements every day of their work life, we have something ... regardless of the condition ... to be thankful for, don't you think?

What about your health?

We all know that person that when you ask them (sincerely and with feeling, of course) how they are doing, he/she ALWAYS responds by telling you the list of all the things wrong with them. Their response usually goes something like this: "Well, my head hurts, my ears are ringing, my stomach's been unsettled, my leg hurts, my bum shoulder has been acting up, and my allergies are kicking my butt."

Please understand that I'm not discounting that person's pain or discomfort. Nor do I doubt what they are saying is true. And I'm certainly not unsympathetic as to the way they are feeling, because nobody likes to have those types of things going on.

What I am saying is that wouldn't it be refreshing if that person ... just once ... responded like this: "Well, I can see your beautiful face, I'm able to walk, I can hear the birds singing, there is breath in my lungs, and I am truly blessed by God to be alive today."

Who wouldn't want to be around that person? Who wouldn't want to engage more with that person? Just try saying that response aloud without feeling good. It's impossible!

**TTA #2:** Before you read any further, put this book down and start counting the things about your health—*whether you deem it good or bad*—you can be thankful for. Begin with the basics ... you can see the words on these pages ... and branch out from there. Take five minutes, though I must warn you, that won't nearly be enough time.

And here is the really interesting part about what you just did. When you practice gratitude, you can't help but feel great. Great about you, great about others, great about your health, and great about life as a whole. Sure, there are things you'd like to be enhanced in your life but being thankful for the positives helps keep the focus off the negatives. If you are not convinced, then try it again and expand what you are thankful for beyond your health.

\*\*\*

Robert Emmons, professor of psychology at the University of California, Davis, is one of the foremost authorities in North America on gratitude. He states the following at http://gratitudepower.net/science.htm:

*Without gratitude, life can be lonely, depressing and impoverished. Gratitude enriches human life. It elevates, energizes, inspires and transforms. People are moved, opened and humbled through expressions of gratitude.*

Do you know somebody who walks around and seemingly never has had a bad moment in their life? You know the type: it's the person who's always smiling; the one telling you to look on the bright side when you're feeling down; and the one who's always glad to tell a story to make others feel good. The next time you see this person, ask them their "secret." Ask them why they're always like that. And why nothing gets them sad. Chances are they'll tell you it's because they are thankful. They realize all that they *do* have and that they feel that a good way to express their gratitude is to be happy and to help others.

They'll also go on to tell you that, of course, they get sad and "life" sometimes bothers them, but their perspective is that, because they have so much … *whether or not others see it this way* … they are able to more quickly move beyond the sadness and disappointments that we all experience.

Also of note is that Jeffrey J. Froh, an assistant professor of psychology at Hofstra University, has uncovered some really interesting information. In an article written in *Psychology Today* titled "Gratitude and Giving Thanks," written by Samantha Smithstein, PsyD, Froh has found that "adults who feel grateful are more optimistic, report more social satisfaction, experience less envy, less depression and fewer physical complaints."

Additionally, he points out, "They also sleep better and get more exercise."

But that's not all.

"What about kids?" you may ask. Is this something that I only, as an adult, should practice and let my kids gain some life experience first? Should I let them develop their own perspective and develop their own gratitude habits when they can better understand what gratitude is all about?

My answer is a resounding, **"NO!"** because as Froh goes on to point out, "Kids who experience more gratitude do better in school, set higher goals for themselves, derive more satisfaction from life, friends, family and school and are generally less materialistic and [have] more desire to give back."

When we think about habits, most people will instantly think of something negative that they do. For example, I smoke, I drink, I use too many swear words, etc. "I can't change," you may exclaim. First of all, I disagree but we'll get more into that in a minute. Second, with regard to your kids, wouldn't it be great to help them practice gratitude early in life? Wouldn't this be a great habit to develop?

Now back to you and your life.

If you feel you "can't change," then try a little experiment for me. If you don't regularly practice gratitude, the question becomes where and how to start. There are a number of different options. One such option includes taking just a few minutes each day to reflect on things you are thankful for. You can do this when you lie in bed after your alarm clock goes off, in the shower, on your way to work, or as part of something you do when you are lying in bed before going to sleep for the night. Talk about setting yourself up for some pleasant dreams.

However, if you are new to this, and want something more concrete, I would recommend going out and investing $1.00 in yourself. Go out to your local Dollar Store, Walmart, or Target and buy a notebook to start journaling. Nothing fancy, just your plain old, everyday notebook.

If you're not familiar with journaling, it's simply the practice of writing out your thoughts and feelings on particular topics and events that you experience in your life. They could be topics that make you happy, sad, frustrated, and/or leave you with feelings of exhilaration. In this case, though, let's make it a "Gratitude Journal."

Which leads me to this:

**TTA #3:** Following your "Commitment of Three", for the next seven days I'd like you to write down five new things each day that you can give thanks for. Five big things or five little things, it doesn't matter. Just make sure it is at least five things.

If you are having a little difficulty figuring out what to write, let me first give an example of what your list should **NOT** look like.

## Things I'm Thankful For

- Family
- Love
- Friends
- Money
- Health

Instead, to really help in feeling your gratitude, I suggest writing it like this.

## Thank You, God, for These Gifts in My Life

1. My family—husband/wife—he/she is the single most important person in my life and I am so thankful for his/her love, support, and kindness. My child(ren) who is/are such a loving soul(s) and who helps make me a better person.
2. Joe—he is my best friend and somebody I know I can always rely on for a smile and help when needed.
3. Health—that allows me to experience life through things such as sight, sound, and thought.
4. Love—thank you for allowing me to have this in my life with my wife, child(ren), parents, brother(s) and sister(s).
5. Money—that allows me to have clothes on my back, food on the table, and a roof over my head.

As you get ready to write for Day 2, read over your previous day's list and do this for each successive day to really help drive home the feelings and allow you to feel the gratitude each and every day. And as we did with giving, take notice and become aware of how you are feeling to truly experience what it is like to give thanks and practice gratitude.

It used to be believed that a new habit took twenty-one days to develop. There are now numerous studies, however, pointing out how a new habit takes, on average, sixty-six days before it becomes part of your everyday life. And while this sounds like a long time, the thing you'll want to focus on is not how short or long something takes, but how it makes you feel along the way. This, my friends, is something that will make you feel good. After all, feeling good is something you and everybody deserves, so enjoy this time. Here is a worksheet that will assist you.

## Thank You, God, for These Gifts in My Life (Day 1)

1._____
2._____
3._____
4._____
5._____

## Thank You, God, for These Gifts in My Life (Day 2)

1._____
2._____
3._____
4._____
5._____

## Thank You, God, for These Gifts in My Life (Day 3)

1._____
2._____
3._____
4._____
5._____

## Thank You, God, for These Gifts in My Life (Day 4)

1._____
2._____
3._____
4._____
5._____

## Thank You, God, for These Gifts in My Life (Day 5)

1._____
2._____
3._____
4._____
5._____

## Thank You, God, for These Gifts in My Life (Day 6)

1._____
2._____
3._____
4._____
5._____

## Thank You, God, for These Gifts in My Life (Day 7)

1._____
2._____
3._____
4._____
5._____

The last thing I'd like to discuss in this chapter is art. Don't worry if you do not possess the talents of a da Vinci or Picasso because the art I'm referencing will not be found in any museum. They won't write a mystery-murder-type movie that centers around the multi-million-dollar painting you've done. Nor will it be the centerpiece of somebody's personal collection.

The art I'm speaking about is the art of letting go.

I'd like you to consider the following: *If you want to grow, you must let go.*

To me, letting go is another way of expressing gratitude because letting go refers to releasing your fears. It's about taking the experiences that have occurred in your life and coming to the understanding that the worst things you've imagined have rarely, if ever, come true. The things that keep you awake, worrying about, tossing and turning for the better part of eight hours. Let them go! The upcoming … and even past … events that cause your stomach to rumble and have it feeling like it's in knots. All that anxiety. Let it go! It's about the stories we all create in our minds … *which always seem to have a negative outcome* … before we even have the chance for the story to play itself out. Let it go! Or at the very least, give them a happy ending.

Have you done this before? Did you do it recently? Today? Don't answer that but tell me if you can relate to the following:

*It's the night before your big presentation. It's happening first thing in the morning and you're heading to bed early for a good night's sleep. You're getting settled for the night, have your cozy pajamas on, make sure your sheets are tucked in the way you like them, brush your teeth, and find that perfect spot in your bed that says, "Ahhhhhhhhhhh."*

*Now logically, you know that you've done all the required work. You know you've rehearsed your speech. And you know that you're prepared to answer any and all questions thrown your way. "Peaceful bliss, here I come," you say to yourself.*

*And just as you're ready to drift off for the night, it happens. Panic sets in!*

*All forms of logic leave you, as question after question plays over and over again in your mind.*

*"What if my PowerPoint doesn't work properly?" "Did I make all the necessary copies for everybody?" "If I blow it, that promotion that I've been working so hard for won't happen." "What if there's something coming out of my nose and nobody pays attention to what I'm saying?" "What if my zipper doesn't stay up and people can see my underwear?" "Will I remember to wear underwear?"*

*Now you're faced with having to calm yourself down and once you do, you realize that you can't get comfortable as you kick the sheets and blankets off. Your cozy spot? Gone! Your pillows suddenly have gone from soft and billowy to rock hard and painful to lay on. You toss. You turn. And your good night's sleep is no more than a wishful thought.*

*The alarm clock mercifully goes off. You're tired and cranky but you know that it's "show time." You get into work, fire up the computer ... and the PowerPoint works fine. You've made an ample number of copies so not only will everybody in the room have one, but you have extras for the executives who weren't able to make the meeting. You've previously stepped into the bathroom so, "Nose clear?" Check! "Zipper up?" Check! And just in case, you've double checked the underwear situation.*

*You give your presentation and really nail it! The only negative being that one of your bosses ... who'll now be one of your colleagues because you've just gotten that promotion ... tells you that you look horrible and should get more sleep.*

Afterward, following all the congratulations, pats on the back, and high-fives, you come to ask yourself one last question, *"What was I so worried about?"*

You knew you'd done this a hundred times before, have always been successful, and that your time was now, to shine like never before. Despite all your efforts, energy, and preparation, you forgot one thing. You forgot to let go and trust and to be thankful for the opportunity. Thankful for being fully prepared. Thankful for the successful presentation ... even before it happened.

*If you want to grow, you must let go.*

Let go of all the negative thoughts and emotions. Leave the fear and worry behind and be thankful for the amazing things that are happening.

The art of expressing gratitude and being thankful are tools that you can apply to all aspects of your life. Not just at work or school, but also when dealing with a family member, friend, or spouse. You can apply it to a short-term goal you've set for yourself ... from weight loss, packing on some muscle, to stopping smoking. And you can apply it to longer-term goals as well ... to live in a bigger house, drive a higher-quality car, or to finally get that swimming pool you've been talking about since you were a kid.

Here, though, in my opinion, is the best way to express gratitude and give thanks—when it is used to help others. Now, there's nothing wrong with any of the other things I've mentioned. In fact, some of them I strive for as well. When you help others, however, you also help yourself—not usually by some material reward you may receive, but in the way you feel about yourself.

Are you seeing a trend here?

Whether it's giving to others or expressing gratitude, not only do you positively impact others, but you positively impact yourself. Sounds like a win-win to me.

## Chapter Three
## Little Changes = BIG Changes

*The man who begins to move a mountain*
*begins by carrying away little stones.*
—Confucius

*It is not the strongest of the species that survives,*
*nor the most intelligent that survives.*
*It is the one that is most adaptable to change.*
—Charles Darwin

Now that we've tackled one of life's biggest questions regarding the meaning of life, let's move on. By now, my hope is that you're getting excited, are conducting the TTAs, and want to know, "What's next?"

My eighty-six-point plan for life-altering change, of course.

Just kidding. I wouldn't do that to you ... or myself.

The fact is, you're already on your way, have adapted a couple of exercises into your routine, and have been noticing change. But I'd like to caution you here. Do not expect miraculous changes in society because of what you've done.

Not yet anyway.

In order to make major, positive, and lasting changes, our undertaking will take time. Theoretically, if everybody read this book at the same time and implemented its recommendations, change in the world would be immediate. The fact is, however, this is not the case. And that's OK.

Let's bring the focus back to you and your efforts because as I'm sure you've already noticed, they are paying dividends.

Are you "pumped up?" Are you "psyched?" Well, you should be. Because by and large, we don't celebrate the positive, little changes in life. If you don't take the time to acknowledge that you are doing something good or worthwhile, perhaps it's because you don't want to come across as if you are bragging.

Let me suggest that this is the next little change you make.

But you may be saying to yourself, *"I've got so much to do yet, I don't want to lose the momentum. I don't want to get ahead of myself."* And I get that because maybe you're afraid that if you say something good, the "goodness" will go away. And like most of you, I consider myself humble and don't want to have people think of me as a bragger or full of myself. But that's not the case with me and I'm sure it's not with you either.

By celebrating the victories in life, though, you give yourself permission to feel good … and this is a feeling we constantly want to have. When we feel good, we want to continue to feel good, and if we continue to feel good, it means we've done something well.

You've heard of a "vicious cycle," right? You know, when one negative thing leads to another and to another, which ultimately leads you back to the original bad thing. It's a feeling that leads you to think you'll never get out of that loop.

Well, let's call this a "Victorious Cycle." Allow yourself to feel good, to smile, to invite others to share your success and help them to feel good … which will help you to feel good, to smile, to invite others to share your success and help them feel good.

Victory!

And this is just one little thing you can do.

What good feelings, smiling, and victorious cycles lead to are a greater feeling for you to grow, to help more people and have more of a positive impact on the lives of others … and potentially a lot of others.

Remember that story I told you about in chapter 1 with one person buying another person breakfast and that growing to at least seven people doing that for another? Well, that one little story, in that one little town made it 700+ miles to me and probably (at least) across the country when those people shared it with others in their circles.

It was a seemingly little thing in that it directly impacted seven people but it led to a big thing easily impacting hundreds, if not thousands, who've read about it (and hopefully now, even more) with people across the United States, and possibly beyond, learning about it.

One person. Doing one little thing. For one single person. Leading to a big thing!

Victory!

But that one story is just that … one story. You see, because we are so inundated throughout the day, every day, with negative, energy-draining news coverage from around the world, it's easy to think of this as the exception.

Actually, though, I believe it's really the rule.

Here's another real-life story you may like. This one is from Jim Barbee of Raleigh, North Carolina. He tells the story about an annual event that has helped create childhood memories that will last a lifetime.

"I love Halloween and this is a love that I'm proud to have passed down to my children. In fact, I've always loved scary movies and as testimony to that, regularly attend the annual Mad Monster Parties held over the course of a weekend in Charlotte. Every year, I transform my yard into a haunted maze that will have parents and their kids from my neighborhood and others in the area come walk through it. It's something me and my kids really enjoy creating.

"But I don't stop there. I use both my front and backyard to really help create a creepy, scary, but overall, fun event for all who come by. I don't charge any money to walk through but I have accepted donations in the past to help a local charity. It's something I'm very proud of, hope that it sends a great message to my children, and look forward to every year. There's nothing like seeing the smile on the kids' (and their parents') faces and because of that, it has become a Barbee family tradition!"

A little thing? To some maybe, but to those kids, it means much more. I mean, think about this. If there was one household in every neighborhood across America that for at least one night (or day) has as its goal to bring joy to (in Jim's case) hundreds of kids, what could that do for the happiness of our society? There are over 19,000 neighborhoods in the United States according to the 2013 Census Bureau and if that event was duplicated and reached 200 kids, we are talking about an impact of 3.8 million kids … plus their parents. If Halloween is not your thing, no worries. You can fashion something around Easter, the Fourth of July, or quite frankly, you can create your own special day.

Little things to us can really mean big things to so many people. We talk about diverse cultures, ethnicities, religions living among us and we understand that we are going to have some differences … differences in our backgrounds, heritage, and even gods … but one thing that should always be known by ALL people is—like the old saying goes—little things mean a lot.

\*\*\*

Would you like to know about another opportunity I've learned about that can positively impact people?

Did you know that $25 could make a profound impact on tens, hundreds, and even thousands of people? And did you further know that this $25 could impact people around the world? Seems like such a small amount to have such a big impact, no?

But it's true.

By making a one-time loan … notice I said "loan" and not "donation" … of as little as $25, you can help people and businesses around the world get the supplies they need to live a healthier life. You can help them get an education or help buy them the supplies they need to run a successful business.

By making a loan through www.Kiva.org, you can make an initial donation of $25, be paid back over a certain time period, and once your money is repaid, donate that same $25 to another person/ family. It's that simple. It's that easy. And it is *that* rewarding.

There is no pressure, no further obligation, and no "have-to's" in doing this. What there is, though, is an overwhelming feeling of satisfaction in making a positive difference in somebody else's life … over and over again … for only the initial $25 you loaned!

And lastly regarding Kiva. I love the thought they share in their "About Us" tab on their website. It states: "We envision a world where all people hold the power to create opportunity for themselves and others."

After all, isn't that all we want? An opportunity.

There are undoubtedly countless stories and organizations around the world that have a positive impact on the lives of others. And while some may look at the examples I gave and call them "small" or "little" in a derogatory way, I would politely point out that they're missing the point. It is truly the little things in life that make the difference.

I mentioned earlier the expression, "Little things mean a lot." There are some people, though, who take this even further, saying that *"little things mean everything."* I believe there's a lot of credence to that statement because while we'd all aspire to do something huge in life like, say, end homelessness, that is a tremendous undertaking for one person.

The facts are that most of us don't have all the necessary resources to be able to accomplish this. However, I suggest that when you take action, even a small action, it is proportionate to what you have. I call this "Proportionate Giving."

For example, most people out there can't donate one million dollars to any one individual or charity because proportionately speaking, our value isn't, say, $100 million. However, most people can donate $20 to a cause and have a positive impact because this is an amount that is comfortable for them, yet still impactful for others.

Proportionate giving.

And since most people would fall into the $20 camp versus the $1 million camp, these seemingly "little" $20 donations add up quickly and mean everything to the receiver.

And as an added bonus, think about what it does for you, the giver. As we discussed earlier, it's not always easy to give any amount, so this should feel good. And really, it should feel great because we have to realize that when we do what we can to help others, we should allow ourselves to feel great about that.

That $20 can make all the difference in the world and while we'd like to give more, we have to make sure that what we give doesn't hurt anybody … including ourselves.

And these little things add up.

But there are still the skeptics out there who'll say, *"Don't you watch the news? I don't care how many little things you do, there are too many negative things happening in the world to make up for them."*

And to those who feel this way, I respectfully say you're wrong!

But don't just take my word for it. Consider what Kenan Distinguished Professor of Psychology at the University of North Carolina at Chapel Hill, Dr. Barbara Fredrickson, said in an interview by Angela Winter titled "The Science of Happiness: Barbara Fredrickson on Cultivating Positive Emotions", originally published in the May 2009 edition of *The Sun*. (https://wintercreativestudio. com/the-science-of-happiness/) Dr. Fredrickson states the following in response to Winter's comment, "I've wondered whether negative stories carry more weight or are simply more compelling":

"Negative events do grab people's attention far more than positive ones. In psychology, this is called the 'negativity bias.' Our brains are wired to scan for perennial threats like the ones our ancestors faced. Yet there's another psychological finding that gets talked about less called 'positivity offset.' It says that even though the negative grabs more attention, most moments in life—if you evaluate them one-by-one—are actually positive. So, the opportunities to experience positive emotions are much more abundant. Indeed, negative emotions grab our attention partly because they're relatively rare in day-to-day living."

As one of my favorite television/movie characters—Ari Gold from *Entourage*—would say, "Boom!"

\*\*\*

The focus thus far, has been on mental and emotional benefits received from practicing giving and gratitude. They include an increased level of happiness and how they inspire and transform people.

In our next chapter, I will address how giving and gratitude will also enhance your physical well-being.

# Chapter Four
# Here's to Your Health

*It is health that is real wealth and not pieces of gold and silver.*
—Mahatma Gandhi

Tell me if this has happened to you.

You're talking with friends or family and somehow the conversation takes a turn to a more serious topic. You've gone from this lighthearted, laughter-filled discussion and all of a sudden, somebody changes the tone by asking a very difficult question. You find yourself thinking and concentrating more because you know you have to give the best answer to this in-depth, possibly life-altering question.

The question?

*If you could have any superpower from any superhero, what would it be?*

Would you like to be able to control the oceans and all marine life like Aquaman? Have the super speed of the Flash? What about one of the powers of Wonder Woman? Batman? Black Panther? Superman? Professor Xavier? So many cool abilities and every person who chooses seems to make a great case for their choice. For the record, I have to go with Superman. I mean, c'mon, is there really anybody who can defeat him?

Have you considered your own superpowers, though? Yes, you! Of course, I'm not speaking of x-ray vision or anything like that. I'm speaking of the incredible powers that giving and gratitude offer. I'm speaking about the health benefits ... *physical, mental, and emotional* ... that practicing giving and being thankful offer. I'm speaking about being more physically fit. I'm speaking about overcoming trauma. I'm speaking about your emotional and psychological health.

Want to lower your blood pressure? Give to others. Want to rid yourself of negative thoughts and emotions? Be thankful. Would you like to have new and different acquaintances and friends? You guessed it, practice giving and gratitude.

*"So if I just say thank you more and drop some loose change in the jar at my convenience store, then I'll overcome my struggles? OK, I'll do it,"* perhaps you find yourself saying. Well, it's not quite that easy. The thing is, you have to combine sincerity with those acts. Truly be thankful. Give your loose change or dollar bills because you *sincerely* want to and not because you now feel you're owed something.

Earlier in the book, I talked about giving (your time, attention, energy, etc.) with no expectations of receiving anything in return. This still holds true. It has to be sincere. It has to be real. It has to be because you truly want to make a difference.

The same thing applies to being thankful. Be thankful for all the positive things and people in your life. Appreciate the good traits. Appreciate the things your possessions can do for you. And would you like to go a little deeper? Then be thankful for the traits of those closest to you that you may find to be challenging to deal with. Appreciate and be thankful for the things you *don't* have.

Do you have what would be considered good, overall health? Be thankful. Do you not enjoy that type of health? Then be thankful for things like being able to read the words on these pages or hear the words as somebody reads it to you.

I say this because when you step back and really look at life, there is so much out there. There are so many different people, for example, with so many different thoughts. Appreciate them. It's not you but it's kind of cool because it allows you perspective. Now I'm not saying to "appreciate" criminal acts, for example, or acts that hurt others, either physically or emotionally. But I am saying to appreciate a difference of opinion, a different course of action in a given situation than you would take.

Let's put some facts behind the thoughts that being thankful and giving to others will help improve your health, shall we? Let's look at giving first.

In an article titled "7 Science-Backed Reasons Why Generosity Is Good for Your Health" that appeared on HuffingtonPost.com dated December 1, 2013, and updated December 6, 2017 (https://www.huffingtonpost.com/2013/12/01/ generosity-health_n_4323727.html), the article's author, Amanda L Chan, wrote: "Researchers from the University of Buffalo found a link between giving and unselfishness and having a lower risk of early death." This study was published in the *American Journal of Public Health*. She goes on to write, "The findings show that helping others—whether it be by helping to run errands, watching their children or giving them a lift somewhere—is linked with a decreased mortality risk."

What about your mental health? The same article points out that "a huge review of 40 studies on the effect of volunteering on general health and happiness was published in the journal *BMC Public Health*. The results? Volunteering not only improves well-being and life satisfaction, but it's also linked with decreased depression and a lower risk of dying early."

In a different article titled "Giving Goes a Long Way: 4 Ways Generosity Positively Impacts Your Health" (https://www. livegenerously.com/inspiring-stories/generosity-health-boost.html) one of the benefits addresses lowering blood pressure and states the following: "According to a study by the Department of Psychology at Carnegie Mellon University, adults who volunteered at least four hours a week were less likely to develop hypertension than those who volunteered less."[4] The article goes on to ask, "What's the connection?" and states, "There are several possible reasons, including the reduction in stress. In fact, when researchers looked at the MRIs of people who gave to various charities, they found that generosity stimulates the reward center in the brain and releases endorphins. Endorphins can help combat stress, which can help prevent many illnesses."[5]

---

4    S. Cohen and R. S. Sneed, "A Prospective Study of Volunteerism and Hypertension Risk in Older Adults," PubMed.gov, June 28, 2013, https://www.ncbi.nlm.nih.gov/pubmed/23795768 (accessed November 25, 2017).

5    Lorie Johnson, "Stress-Free: Heal Yourself with Generosity," CDN News, November 24, 2015. http://www1. cbn.com/cbnnews/healthscience/2014/june/stress-free-heal-yourself-with-generosity (accessed November 25, 2017).

When you stop and think about it, I believe most people can (begrudgingly in some cases) get behind the fact that the act of giving would lead to at least some benefits. But what about gratitude? Can being thankful *really* lead to improved health?

Let's take a look at some interesting facts about practicing gratitude.

An article appearing in *Psychology Today*, "7 Scientifically Proven Benefits of Gratitude," by Amy Morin, the author lists the following as the seven benefits: (https://www.psychologytoday. com/us/blog/what-mentally-strong-people-dont-do/201504/7-scientifically-proven-benefits-gratitude)

1) Gratitude opens the door to more relationships;
2) Gratitude improves physical health;
3) Gratitude improves psychological health;
4) Gratitude enhances empathy and reduces aggression;
5) Grateful people sleep better;
6) Gratitude improves self-esteem; and
7) Gratitude increases mental strength.

"Dimension and Perspectives of Gratitude," written by Dr. Robert Emmons and Dr. Michael McCullough, point to a number of benefits one receives in showing an attitude of gratitude. The authors conclude:

> In an experimental comparison, those who kept gratitude journals on a weekly basis exercised more regularly, reported fewer physical symptoms, felt better about their lives as a whole, and were more optimistic about the upcoming week compared to those who recorded hassles or neutral life events.

and

> Grateful people report higher levels of positive emotions, life satisfaction, vitality, optimism and lower levels of depression and stress. The disposition toward gratitude appears to enhance pleasant feeling states more than it diminishes unpleasant emotions. Grateful people do not deny or ignore the negative aspects of life.

Wow! Of all the things we can be, of all the emotions we carry around, of all the thoughts that run in and out of our minds, simply by sincerely being thankful and giving to others we receive two— *now proven*—ways to improve our health. It improves the way we feel both physically and mentally! It improves our outlook on life! It reduces stress!

As I stated earlier, "Wow!"

\*\*\*

There was a statement in the last study from Drs. Emmons and McCullough that really caught my attention. They found, "Grateful people do not deny or ignore the negative aspects of life." I think that is a major key to understanding the mindset of those who regularly practice G & G. It's not that those who've made giving and gratitude a consistent part of their lives walk around thinking that the world is perfect and things couldn't possibly get better. On the contrary. They recognize the events that are taking place, the seemingly accepted "snarkiness" that is consistently tweeted or posted and given so much attention. It's just that they try and focus their attention more on the good things in life, the uplifting quotes shared, and the positive events that are happening all around them. It's not that there is a blind eye turned to what's happening, but, on a personal level, I aspire to being aware of what's going on, but not to allow myself to be overwhelmed, when speaking about the constant barrage of bad news and current events being reported. If this advice is put into action, people are aware of events happening but don't allow those events to bring them down to a level where they don't care or think that they can't make a difference.

It comes down to perspective, which is quite possibly my favorite word. Perspective has to do with the way you look at a given situation. A very common example to consider, "Is the glass half full or half empty?" I've always considered myself a glass half full person until I read these words: "It doesn't matter if the glass is half-full or half-empty. Be thankful that you have a glass and there is something in it."

Perspective. Here are a couple more.

In business, when you come across an employee who's been with the company for twenty, thirty years or more, do you see him/

her as somebody who's out of touch with the way things work today or somebody who has a lot of great experiences and stories you can learn from? That also works the other way around in that if you are that veteran in a particular job or industry, are you open to newer, different approaches? Or, are you more of the mindset that says, *"Why change? We've always done it this way."*

Perhaps you're still in school. Are you the type that if you take a 50-question test and get 48 of the questions correct, are you excited about the 96% you scored ... an A+ ... the highest grade you can possibly get ... or for the next couple of day, do you focus on the two questions you got wrong?

Perspective is a very funny thing. It gives a person great insight as to how another thinks. It is also vital when discussing giving and gratitude, especially when it comes to one's health.

Do you know who K. C. Mitchell is? I learned of his story from a number of sources including *Athlete Daily* and *Muscle & Fitness*. K. C. is a powerlifter. He weighs 240 pounds and can deadlift 606 pounds. He does this while being unable to completely close his right hand. He has five screws, ruptured meniscus on both sides of his right knee, and ankle pins in the same leg. This former army staff sergeant is on a mission, though. That is to become the strongest nonadaptive amputee lifter in the world.

Oh, did I forget to mention that he had his left leg amputated while on his second tour of duty (less than one week away from ending) when his vehicle struck a land mine?

He admits to having numerous challenges and struggles along the way but ultimately, he has built his body and mind to a point where he now gives motivational talks and points to being able to change people's lives as a big motivating factor.

Talk about giving to others. He could have easily just gone about his business, got his life together, and lifted to get stronger, but that wasn't enough. He took to Instagram, shared his journey ... including the many difficulties he's battled ... and on the other side, despite his troubles and losing his leg, he has gone on to improve his life and countless others around the world. Awesome job, K. C.!

Let's look at another example. This time, let's focus on your emotional health and a different kind of giving. Oftentimes, when people excel at their jobs, they have the opportunity to get promoted and move up the "corporate ladder." You're now entrusted to do more and, excitedly, get an increase in your pay. It's a great feeling to be recognized in this way, knowing that your hard work and dedication has paid off, not to mention the level of respect you've more than likely earned from your peers.

In the case when you have a family, there are some other things that come with that promotion. Longer days may bleed into the night, for one. You may also find that you need to work on the weekends to stay ahead. This opportunity may also come with an increase in overnight travel. A day or two here and there is one thing, but multiple times during a given month means another.

Your emotions teeter because, on the one hand, your hard work is paying off and it feels really, really good, and the pride that comes with that feeling is hard to match. But on the other hand, your family and the dynamic you've become accustomed to changes as well. Your spouse, who may also work, now has to pick up on at least some of the responsibilities you typically handled. And you also run the risk of not being around as often for your kids and their activities.

You may wrestle with this decision because again, in weighing the pros and cons, you realize that there are more things you may be able to do with the added income. You may be able to finally get that new car that you need, take a family vacation every year, or perhaps even get a larger, roomier home.

Then the other side jumps into your mind. *"Yeah, but am I being fair to my spouse?"* you ask yourself. And what about your kids? *"They're at that age where I know they need me, not to mention, how much I would miss not being available for them,"* your counterpoint chimes in.

Is your marriage and relationship with your children strong enough? Is the financial need that great that you have to try? And here's a biggie, are *you* strong enough to make the change? These are all questions that may enter your mind.

Here's the thing about this situation. There is no one right answer that applies to everybody. There is only the right answer that applies to you and your situation. And while I believe it is important to include your spouse in this decision, this ultimately comes down to how you're going to feel about it … emotionally. Is there more value (non-financially) to be around more for your family and keep things as they are? Will the changes in your dynamic at home be overcome by being able to earn more money and live a more comfortable life? Again, only you can answer these questions. However, giving in this way, whether accepting or not accepting this promotion, I feel, will go a long way toward your overall emotional health.

Lastly, you may feel that this is an opportunity that may never come again. And while you may be correct about this specific opportunity, I want you to understand it's not the last one. In the next chapter, we'll discover why having this one particular characteristic will assure you of a lifetime of chances to improve upon any given situation.

# Chapter Five
# Limitless Opportunities

*When you give of yourself and practice gratitude,*
*the mind expands to the point of genuinely understanding*
*that you are limitless.*

I had a tremendously exciting job opportunity a few years back. This opportunity would allow me to essentially learn about an industry I was thrilled about, help others, and help myself and my family with a generous compensation package. It would involve me being able to visit work sites in countries I've always wanted to visit, such as Amsterdam.

The job came down to me and three others and a final interview. As I was parking my car, I remembered to pop in my Eminem CD that had the song "Lose Yourself" on it. That song was featured in his 2002 movie, *8-Mile*. It was a song I had played prior to every phone and in-person interview I had had up to that point with this company and since I had gotten this far ... *and, yes, I can be a bit superstitious as you'll find out in chapter 8* ... I wasn't going to stop now.

Part of the song included the lyrics, *"This opportunity comes once in a lifetime."*

As much as I liked the entire song, it's that line that always got to me. It's what always stuck in my mind in the song. At the time, I truly felt that this was my chance, my shot, and I'd never have another opportunity this good.

By now I'm sure you guessed that I did not get the job. I was the runner-up. They went with another gentleman who had industry experience. Honestly, though, I also feel another determining factor was that I don't feel it was my best interview.

Talk about being bummed out.

Everything was falling in place, my kids were a bit older, my marriage was as strong as ever (so the concerns of the last chapter weren't there), and I was going to leave an industry that I was beginning to tire of. My salary would jump significantly with the chance to earn on top of that. I'd get to travel to different parts of the world (and was planning on sneaking my wife in on a trip or two as well), and I'd be doing something that I was genuinely excited about. One shot … and I blew it.

But did I?

Was this my one and only shot, really? I was in my late thirties at the time, so was this it? Back to what I was doing with no other chance ever again to get what I wanted?

While I was understandably disappointed as I know most people would be, boy, was I being short-sighted. Because the thing is, nothing changed. I was still blessed in so many ways. There were so many things to be thankful for. I still had my amazing wife and daughters in my life. I was still young, excited about life, and healthy. I still got to drive around in my company car and work in an industry that likewise allowed me to genuinely help people and positively impact a number of lives.

I could look at things one of two ways: (1) I blew it and nothing this good will ever come along again, which would probably put me in a very long funk about life; or (2) Well, I didn't get this job, but look at all the things I still have. I get to interact with some amazing people, and I get to set myself up to dream about other possibilities down the road.

Other possibilities? Yes! And plenty of them. Because while I didn't get that job with all the exciting aspects I outlined, it allowed me to meet new people here, plus develop new relationships and strengthen so many existing ones. It's allowed me to ultimately get back into my first love … baseball … and serve as a middle school and high school coach. It allowed me to discover a new passion in helping others—motivational speaking—and put into action newer and bigger dreams.

All because of something that *didn't* happen.

How many people do you think can relate to a story like mine? I know through family and friends alone that some of the best things that have happened *to them* are the things that didn't happen *for them*. You've heard of "a blessing in disguise," right? How apropos in this example.

What about you? What story in your life came to mind? How did you act? React?

*"Whether you think you can or think you can't, you're right."* This quote by Henry Ford has always struck a chord with me because I'm a big believer in the power of your thoughts. That ability to will yourself through a given situation is something I've long believed in. I incorporated this thought to help me find my way back to being positive and having optimism for my life.

While this quote has always been one of my favorites, with all due respect to Henry Ford, I feel there is something lacking within it. Lots of people dream and I feel that is fantastic. We have to have something that gets us excited, that we can hold onto, and allow us to escape our day-to-day reality.

But what about action? If you want a dream to become your reality, taking action to make it so is a necessity. Without action, it will always remain a dream. And if that's what you desire, to just dream and imagine, then I'm all for it. However, if you're looking to take that next step in life, whether it's about finding that special someone, advancing in your career, starting your own company, or simply being a kinder person, I would like to introduce you to a new term. It's really a thought process and one I've developed over the past few years.

First a question. Do you consider yourself to be smart? *"Well, sure, I'm a pretty intelligent person,"* you may reply. And while I don't disagree with your answer, I'm speaking about a different kind of smart. Book smart? Street smart? No, not those kinds of "smart" either.

The smart I'm referring to is an acronym that's at the heart and soul of what I believe. It will assist you in accomplishing all that life has to offer once you fully believe and act upon those beliefs. SMART stands for **S**uccess **M**eans **A**cquiring **R**ight Thoughts™ because I fully believe that with the right way of thinking … and, here's the key, *taking action* … you will, without exception, be able to create your reality!

Being SMART in this capacity opens your mind to a world of new and exciting possibilities. It allows you to be in complete and total control. It allows you to dream big, perhaps like never before, and generates excitement, passion, and a thought process geared toward achieving results.

It provides you a lifetime of limitless opportunities!

Each and every day you are fortunate enough to wake up, you have before you an opportunity to make lasting and impactful change in your life and the lives of others. And the next day, you get to do it all over again. It doesn't matter what day of the week it is. It doesn't matter what else you have going on in your life. Your work schedule, lack of free time, and other challenges you face are now looked at through fresh eyes because your thought process has changed.

To help get you in this frame of mind, have you considered turning inward? Another one of my favorite quotes is *"If I don't go within, I go without."* This has been attributed to Neale Donald Walsch, Yogi Bhajan, and a whole host of others. It focuses on sitting quietly in meditation, with the result oftentimes becoming better informed about your true, inner thoughts and feelings. Meditation is a time that also has many tell of how answers to questions they've struggled with, reveal themselves. For me, it comes in the form of a soundless voice, that when sitting quietly, reveals answers that help me move forward. It sets me at ease. And it makes me feel more confident in the actions taken.

There are a number of studies that link meditation to positive outcomes for those who suffer from an abundance of physical and emotional problems. Included among those are pain, high blood pressure, irritable bowel syndrome, depression, anxiety, and insomnia. There is also a 2014 study from the Norwegian University of Science and Technology (NTNU) titled "This is Your Brain on Meditation: Brain Processes More Thoughts, Feelings During Meditation." In part it states, "Nondirective meditation allows for more room to process memories and emotions than during concentrated meditation," says a coauthor of the study. Nondirective meditation is when the person who is meditating effortlessly focuses on his or her breathing or on a meditation sound, but beyond that the mind is allowed to wander as it pleases. This is versus concentrative meditation where the meditating person focuses attention on his or her breathing or on specific thoughts, and in doing so, suppresses other thoughts.

I can't begin to tell you the number of times I've had solutions to problems or issues in my life just seemingly come out of the blue during meditation. Things I haven't consciously thought about in weeks or months but on some level were still present and, suddenly, solved. It is a truly amazing feeling. As Carl Jung once said, "Your visions will become clear only when you can look inside your own heart. Who looks outside, dreams; Who looks inside, awakes."

\*\*\*

I'm not one to argue the science behind this regarding the "memories" and "emotions" cited above; however, there is a different theory and one I ascribe to. That "soundless voice" is considered by many to be your soul speaking to you. You may know soul food. You may know your soul sister. But do you actually know your soul? The soul has a number of definitions attached to it, all pretty similar. Here, though, is my favorite. It comes from the website Catholic.com (https://www.catholic.com/qa/what-exactly-is-a-soul). "Soul" refers to the innermost aspect of man, that which is of greatest value in him, that by which he is most especially in God's image: "Soul" signifies the *spiritual principle* in man. Think about that for a moment. Your soul … talking to you … without a voice. Helping you. Guiding you. Steering you in the right direction. Wanting nothing but the best for you in your life.

Back in chapter 3, you'll recall we discussed "Victorious Cycles." I can't think of a more victory-filled, beautiful cycle than to feed your soul with a quietness that allows it to reveal to you answers to some of your life's biggest problems … which creates a greater desire to continue being quiet … which provides you more and more answers …

Being quiet creates this beautiful, soundless voice that will guide you to greater peace, confidence, harmony, and genuineness as to who you really are.

Meditation in its many forms to me is nothing short of spectacular.

So, what does being SMART and turning inward have to do with giving?

Absolutely everything!

You see, when discussing giving, you also have to give to that one very important person in your life. You. Give yourself the gift of confidence … in yourself, your abilities, your creativeness, your willingness to get things done. Give yourself the gift of faith … in yourself, in others' desires to help you, and in knowing that God has put you on this track of excelling in your life like never before. The gift of understanding in a deeper and more spiritual way is a gift you can give to yourself. You can accomplish this by sitting quietly in a meditative state, and do it in as little as ten minutes a day.

You can also practice visualization, a form of mediation. Visualization is when you see the outcome of something you desire having happened before steps are taken to make it so. However, for visualization to be even more effective, it's not enough to just see the outcome. You want to allow yourself to hear what that accomplishment sounds like. To feel your feelings. To smell what it might smell like. And to readily accept that you have achieved your specific goals.

For example, let's say you decide you want to get yourself in better shape. You sit quietly and see your ultimate goal being achieved. You've now lost twenty pounds, have firmed up your arms, legs, abs, chest, back, shoulders, and let's not forget, you've now got buns of steel. And that's a great start. But now take yourself deeper and hear the "whir" of the elliptical machine, the birds singing on your morning walk, the clanging of the weights, the beads of sweat dripping off the end of your nose and the sound it makes when it hits the floor.

And let's not forget the accolades being heaped upon you when you see family and friends for the first time in a while. You want to "feel the burn" as they used to say, but more importantly, you want to feel the emotions of pride and accomplishment in achieving your goal. Now smell that achievement. If you want to keep it lighthearted, then, yes, smell the stinky, sweaty odor of your clothes. However, also take in the smell of the beach, and totally feel that internal exhilaration when you take off your shirt, because you are now a more confident version of yourself.

Can it really be that simple, though? Can you achieve a long-desired goal just by visualizing yourself accomplishing it?

If you're skeptical as I once was, then consider this. In research done by Harvard University titled "Flexing Your Finger in Your Mind," researchers discovered that people in one group who physically flexed their finger for a length of time over the course of a number of weeks noticed an increase in the strength of that finger. When compared to a group who just visualized flexing the same finger over the course of the same length of time and weeks, the results were astounding.

The group who physically flexed their finger were shown to have a 53 percent increase in the strength of that finger. As for the group who only visualized conducting the same movement with the same finger, the strength in their finger increased by 35 percent. Thirty-five percent! All because they visualized themselves as having physically done the exercise.

What does all of this have to do with gratitude? See my previous answer … absolutely everything!

Be thankful for the situation you now find yourself in. For the positive things, of course, but also for the challenges that lie in front of you. For the new thoughts and dreams that may now enter your mind. For the new people you'll come across. For the obstacles. And most importantly, for how amazing you'll feel when you've come to realize that they were all part of the journey!

The bottom line is this.

Y-O-U, in every possible way, are limitless! You have been blessed with this incredible gift we call life. Like us all, in various forms, you face challenges. But you also have the abilities to see them as opportunities. And, you have the ability to conquer them in every possible facet imagined!

Y-O-U are this beautiful creature that God has created. He didn't create you to struggle. He didn't create you to muddle through life. He created you to excel, to be that highest version of yourself that you've imagined!

\*\*\*

Let me close the chapter with this thought and question for you:

If every person has a soul, and the soul is a piece of God, then every person has a piece of God inside them. Understanding that you and God are one, is there really anything you cannot accomplish?

# Y-O-U ARE LIMITLESS!

# Chapter Six
# Corporate America, Corporate Change

*Gratitude is a currency we can mint for ourselves,*
*and spend without fear of bankruptcy.*
—Fred De Witt Van Amburgh

"I am not a role model."

Those words by former NBA superstar and Hall of Famer Charles Barkley were spoken over twenty-five years ago. That 1993 television commercial for Nike has sparked a number of conversations over the past two and one-half decades regarding whether or not athletes should be considered role models in our society. While Barkley would point out such things in the commercial as "Parents should be role models" and "Just because I dunk a basketball, doesn't mean I should raise your kids," the other side would chime in saying that because he's in the public spotlight and people, especially kids, look up to him, he and other professional athletes have a responsibility to be a role model and act accordingly.

Both sides make good cases. Personally, I see each belief because while I agree that professional athletes should be held to the same standards for living their lives as you and me, I also feel that because they are in the public spotlight, there is a responsibility to act accordingly.

Role model? No. Parents like myself should appreciate that he and the ad point out that we're the ones who should be the role models. Responsible and respectful in the public eye? Absolutely. Like it or not, there are so many children that look up to pro athletes for their talent and work ethic that I believe you have to take on the responsibility that comes with the territory.

Here's another question to consider. Do companies and corporations have a responsibility to set an example for society? Should they be at the forefront on topics including giving and gratitude?

Though justifiable due to a number of instances, companies are under a microscope today for certain behaviors. In a number of these cases, this was self-inflicted through poor decisions regarding policies, marketing, and/or actions taken by company personnel, including the company's leaders. While there is a cynical side that a lot of people have that says any "good" they do is strictly for PR and not because they actually care, there are also a number of companies who are doing some wonderful things, not just with the products or services they offer, but also with their employees and community.

Whether you're looking at major corporations or small "mom-and-pop" types of businesses, you'd be hard-pressed to not be able to find some sort of charitable or philanthropic work they do. That may mean being part of the Adopt-A-Highway program in their part of the country or donating time at a seasonal event such as Operation Christmas Child. It can include food drives in the office, helping a person who is down on his/her luck with money collected from employees, or donating office furniture to a local college's business program.

Whatever it is, whenever they do it, and for whatever reason, people benefit through their giving. And while I think any sort of giving is fantastic, I'd like to point out a few businesses and individuals that do some really wonderful things as they relate to giving and gratitude. They've taken on some of the more traditional types of giving and elevate them to the next level. They've even utilized gratitude. I will mention some by name and highlight many companies that have done this particularly well.

They are the companies that have asked the questions, *"What else can we do? How can we go over and above? How can we raise the bar?"*

I call these amazing companies, ***G&G Corporate All-Stars.***

These companies may partake in activities such as those I presented above but they also do some pretty cool things that I invite other companies to imitate or expand upon in some capacity. What I will highlight in the coming pages sets these companies a notch above because of their creativeness and sincerity in wanting to do something new and exciting.

## G&G Corporate All-Stars #1–#3—CEOs

Gratitude at your place of business seems like a simple enough thing. After all, it's easy to say thank you, to smile and nod in appreciation. How many people, though, take the time and effort in going the extra mile at work to express their thanks?

There are a number of ways people can accomplish this. For example, as a worker, you can volunteer to go in early or stay late although there is no extra pay involved. As somebody who oversees employees, a department, or a company as a whole, you can pay a higher wage or allow a worker who has done a good job to get some extra time at lunch or even give an extra day off. Because of the dedication of your employees as a whole, you may even choose to pay a higher percentage of healthcare costs, which in and of itself would constitute a raise in pay.

I'd like to address an opportunity that is rarely utilized anymore. It is one that costs nothing, can be used by co-workers, leaders, executives, company presidents, and members of your board of directors. In fact, it's well documented that it is a means that has been utilized by Mark Zuckerberg of Facebook and by the CEO of Campbell's Soup, Douglas Conant. Indra Nooyi, the twelve-year CEO of Pepsi Co. who stepped down from her role in 2019, took it even further than the first two, as I'll touch on later.

I'm speaking about the handwritten thank-you note.

I know, I know, your handwriting is so bad that although you've thought of it, you're too embarrassed to ever hand-write anything again. Let me tell you a story about a guy who has bad handwriting and how he overcame that stigma.

Whether it's his wife who has trouble understanding what he's written or if he has difficulty reading his own handwriting, it makes no difference. He may have the situation where two minutes after he wrote himself a note, he can't understand what he has written.

To overstate the obvious, this guy's handwriting is bad. It's sloppy, and even though he got gold star after gold star in elementary school for his cursive writing during penmanship class, he has seemingly forgotten all the rules that he had learned.

As I'm sure you've figured out by now, of course the guy I'm talking about is … my best friend growing up, Mike Hood.

No, that's not true.

It's me. I (finally) admit it and to what will be my wife's pleasure, can never deny it again. I mean it's rancid. But do you want to know a secret? I've discovered that on the occasions I actually slow down the process and remember my lessons from yesteryear, my handwriting is actually legible. So much so that you don't even have to strain your eyes or go back and try to read it a second time.

In getting back to the point, what does a handwritten note say to people? It says you care. It tells them that they're worth the extra time. It tells them that they're worth more than the standard, "Thank You." It lets them know that they are appreciated in a way that goes beyond the norm.

The great thing about a handwritten note is that it doesn't have to come from just a boss or CEO. It can come from a salesman to the warehouse worker, from one customer service representative to another. And if done properly—that is, without having to wipe off a bit of brown from your nose—it can also be done from a worker to the boss.

In fact, if you're looking to create a company culture that lives and breathes gratitude, consider adopting this approach. One that lets people know that they are appreciated. One that has people striving toward receiving that appreciative nod, the high-five, or that handwritten note from the boss or co-worker.

But what about higher pay? Certainly, that's what people really want most, isn't it? No. In fact, appreciation and recognition consistently rank above pay in survey after survey taken on the subject of what's most important to employees.

So how did Indra Nooyi take things a step further? Well, not only did she send handwritten thank-you notes to her employees as Mark Zuckerberg and Douglas Conant do, but she sent them to the worker's parents as well.

If you are a worker who were to receive such a note, how much of an impact would it have on you?

\*\*\*

I've researched a number of giving models utilized by companies that I wanted to feature in this chapter. To say it was difficult to narrow it down is an understatement as there really are a number of companies that do a lot of great work regarding their charitable and giving ways. I didn't want to focus on one while leaving some others out.

Instead I decided to focus on the "why" regarding the reason companies do what they do. My thoughts kept coming back to one company in particular. It's a company that was born in the mid-2000s and rapidly became a household name. Their reputation remains strong to this day as they still make a great product while impacting people worldwide. They began to change the mindset of how a business can have an impact on so many others ... not because of the products they sell ... but because of the products they give.

### G&G Corporate All-Stars #4–#18—Having a Worldwide Impact

Do you know who Blake Mycoskie is? You may not know the name, but you definitely know his company, TOMS. In his book, *Start Something That Matters*—a truly motivating read—he tells the story of how he was inspired to start his company and as its "Chief Shoe Giver"—his official title—he wanted to inspire others.

The story of TOMS (**Tom**morrow's **S**hoes) is an amazing one, highlighting how the idea of giving a pair of shoes away for every pair purchased was born, and the revolution it ultimately began.

Normally when you read about a "revolution," it doesn't involve giving to others as its main premise. However, with the TOMS business model out there for the world to see, other companies adopted the way they do business.

The "Buy One, Give One" is a fantastic model that TOMS—the Godfather ... as I like to call them ... of buy one, give one, revolutionized that has led others to do the same. Here is a list with a brief description as written by Shawn Donnelly on RealClearLife. com in an article titled "16 Brands That Use TOMS Model of One-for-One Giving." The numbers quoted were as of the time of this article.

**TOMS**—*www.TOMS.com*—*shoes, bags, sunglasses, apparel. They also sell/donate coffee, insulated bottles, and t-shirts.*

**One World Play Project**—*www.OneWorldPlayProject.com*—*indestructible soccer balls. Also, durable dog toys. Since 2008, they have distributed over 1,000,000 balls.*

**Bixbee**—*www.Bixbee.com*—*backpacks, lunch boxes, and duffel bags, mostly for kids. They have dozens of backpack styles to choose from.*

**Bombas**—*www.Bombas.com*—*socks for men, women, and children. Over 5,000,000 pairs have been donated.*

**Roma**—*www.RomaBoots.com*—*boots for women and children. They are also sold at hundreds of retailers throughout the United States.*

**Smile Squared**—*www.SmileSquared.com*—*toothbrushes, travel journals, and zippered pouches. They also help fund "wish trips" for children facing life-threatening medical conditions.*

**SoapBox**—*www.SoapBoxSoaps.com*—*bar soap, hand soap, body wash, and hair care products. Started by a college student in 2010, over 1,000,000 donations have been made.*

**Figs**—*www.WearFigs.com*—*medical scrubs and casual clothing for men and women. They've donated nearly 100,000 sets of medical scrubs to developing countries.*

**Better World Books**—*www.BetterWorldBooks.com*—*new and used books. They've raised over $18 million and diverted in excess of 73,000 tons of books from landfills.*

**State**—*www.StateBags.com*—*backpacks, tote bags, and accessories. The backpacks are named after Brooklyn neighborhoods.*

**Project 7**—*www.Project7.com*—*chewing gum and gummies. A sampler pack includes twelve packs of gum. Proceeds from the* *candy are used to fund a number of programs such as feeding the hungry and healing the sick.*

**Out of Print Clothing—www.OutOfPrintClothing.com**—*book-themed clothing, mugs, and tote bags. They fund literacy programs and book donations in underserved communities.*

**Kutoa—www.Kutoa.com**—*health bars. The company promotes healthy living while helping fund programs to feed children around the world.*

**WeWood—www.We-Wood.com**—*wooden watches. And also, glasses. For every timepiece sold, they plant a tree. Since 2011, they've planted in excess of 420,000 trees.*

**This Bar Saves Lives—www.ThisBarSavesLives.com**—*health bars. This "bee-friendly" bar has donated over 3,500,000 packets of life-saving nutrition.*

**Warby Parker—www.WarbyParker.com**—*eyeglasses and sunglasses. They also have over forty stores around the United States that also sells books and other products.*

**Twice As Warm—www.TwiceAsWarm.com**—*hats, scarves, and gloves. They also sell infinity scarves, a very popular item.*

In choosing these companies, it's important to note that the article I referenced was written over two years ago and all the links to the company's websites are still up and running. This means that this particular model is highly effective and one that would be a wonderful idea to consider for new companies that are in the planning process. To those more established companies throughout the world, I'd ask you to consider having part of your business model designed to give more.

*\*\*\**

Earlier in the chapter I asked the question as to whether companies have a responsibility to set an example for society as it relates to giving and gratitude. My answer is a resounding, "Yes!" and I'll explain why. Companies, regardless of size and much like athletes, are in the spotlight today like never before. When you consider the Internet and social media, along with the "gotcha" moments that some people look to capitalize on when companies do something wrong, it has become even more important that companies present themselves in a positive light.

The key to any positive event or identity you present becoming a success, however, is to take whatever action you're partaking in and do it with authenticity. To do it in a way that allows you (the company) to be true to you and your identity ... as we'll discuss in chapter 8. A couple of things come to mind though. While it's true that you can fake sincerity (at least for a little while), the question I would ask is, *"Why would you want to?"*

Whether you are a leader of a department, leader of a district, leader of a region, or are a CEO of a Fortune 500 company, I implore you to take a step back and examine what you've done to date ... *and as I've already pointed out, a number of companies do a lot of things really well* ... and ask you to consider how you can make things better. Is there some form of giving that you can expand on within your company? Are there causes that you'd like to become part of but just haven't seemed to have the time for? Is there something within your town that will allow you to make a positive impact on its people?

What about gratitude? Can you follow the lead of those CEOs I referenced? Is this a platitude—*a platitude of gratitude*—that you can teach and grow within your office and among your employees? Can you do something to say "thank you" to customers in a different way than, say, a coupon? Or if it is a coupon, does it have to be that the customer has to spend $50.00 before they can get $5.00 or $10.00 off?

What about combining the two? Wouldn't it be awesome if you spearheaded a campaign that said "thank you" to those in your community by providing resources to build a new park, for example? I understand that some companies already do things like this and I applaud them for it, but now is the time where, collectively, we can take bigger and bolder steps. It is a time when more companies and their employees can take action to truly impact an even greater number of people in their communities.

If you see more pressing needs on a regional, national, or global scale, there are a number of companies out there you can partner with who have already done the legwork. For example, there are organizations such as Charity: Water (www.CharityWater.org), the National Coalition for the Homeless (www.NationalHomeless. org) and World Food Programme (www.WFP.org).

Why does this all matter? It matters ... and I don't believe this can be overstated ... because we have to get back to being our true selves. We have to get back to listening to that voice inside your head and that feeling in your heart (your soul) that tells you to do more, to be better, and as Gandhi said, *"To be the change you wish to see in the world."*

*\*\*\**

Are you part of, or do you know of, a company you'd like to nominate as a G&G All Star? If so, please e-mail me and let me know about the great work they are doing. My e-mail address is at the back of the book.

# Chapter Seven
# Flash Those Pearly Whites...
# Impact a Life

*Every time you smile at someone, it is an action of love.*
*A gift to that person. A beautiful thing.*
—Mother Teresa

I love the above quote from Mother ... now Saint ... Teresa. It speaks about something that is so commonplace, yet so undervalued. Your smile. It is an expression that is uniquely you, a piece of who you are, and it is something that you can give away over and over again, each and every day. There should be no worries if your teeth aren't perfect or if your smile is crooked, as long as it comes with a sincere genuineness, it will impact others and truly be the "gift" that Mother Teresa spoke of.

When and where you give that gift can sometimes be a challenge. If, for example, you're walking by somebody, flash a nice grin, and are ignored, don't take it personally. Not everybody is so quick to reciprocate for their own reasons, as they may be going through something at that time in their life. For example, they may have gotten some bad news about their job, received word of an illness in the family, or are simply having a bad day. If that's the case, don't let it deter you because you may have impacted that person more than you realize.

Another reason may also be a matter of geography.

I love New York. As I stated earlier, it is where I am originally from and lived for the first twenty-three years of my life. Despite what people from outside of there hear about it, New York is filled with kind, friendly, good-hearted people. We just have a different way of expressing it than, say, in North Carolina, where I have resided since.

In North Carolina, people will typically look right at you, give a friendly smile and a "Hey" to go along with it. In New York, you have to work a little harder because even making eye contact with somebody else can be a challenge. It is just something that most people grew up hearing. "Don't make eye contact with people" was often the refrain I heard as a kid.

Recently, I was in New York and decided to conduct an experiment. Every person I walked by in the street ... and for those of you who don't live there or haven't visited, that's a lot of people ... I was going to engage them. It didn't matter that they had their heads down or would look everywhere else but at me, I was going to see how my greeting would impact them. Young or old, man or woman, I was going to see what type of impact my greeting, eye contact, and of course, smile, would have.

The results?

They were pretty amazing, though not surprising to me. When I'd say, *"Good morning"* or *"Beautiful day, isn't it?"* people would look up and respond. For the ones I smiled at when saying it (everybody), they smiled back. While some were briefly surprised I had greeted them at all—and smiled no less—they were quick to give a response and smile back to me. Every person? No. The vast majority of people? Yes!

While this experiment of mine was hardly scientific, it did go a long way to showing that when you present yourself in a kind, friendly way, most people are not only more receptive to you but will also respond in kind.

To put some science behind the premise, consider the 2002 Swedish study done by Sonnyb-Borgstrom titled *Automatic Mimicry Reactions as Related to Differences in Emotional Empathy*, published in NCBI (National Center for Biotechnology Information). The study's author worked with participants who were shown pictures of different emotions including joy, fear, anger, and surprise. When participants were told to frown when shown a smiling person, however, according to the article titled "Why You Need to Smile More" that appeared on *NeuroNation* (https://www.neuronations. com/science/benefits-of-smiling), they echoed the emotions of the people rather than following the instruction.

My translation is that it is very hard for people to not smile after having received one. Conduct your own experiment, no matter where you live, and try it out for yourself.

But is it really a fact that a smile is a gift? What possible good can come from something that takes less than one second? Well, try accomplishing anything from start to finish, in one second. Chances are, you won't even be able to determine your first step in that time, let alone take it and then complete it. To answer the question, though, anything that requires giving something to another is a gift whether it is something that requires a monetary investment or a simple investment of yourself.

What about making an investment in yourself? Can Mother Teresa's quote also be translated as giving a gift to yourself? Can the life you're impacting be your own?

You bet!

According to many sources and studies, including those by the Chopra Center, Scientific American, Benefits Bridge, Wayne State University, and the Mayo Clinic, the following are listed as health benefits for the person giving out smiles:

1) **Smiling May Help You Live Longer**—Photos of 230 baseball players were studied. They found that players with partial smiles lived two years longer than those who didn't smile. Those who had the biggest smiles lived roughly seven years longer than those who didn't smile.

2) **Smiling Improves Your Relationships**—Studies show that different areas of the brain light up when looking at pictures of people who are smiling versus not smiling. A smile of any degree, it was found, were labeled as more attractive.

3) **Smiling Improves Effectiveness in the Workplace**— Smiling at your co-workers creates moments of connection that lead to greater productivity and teamwork. Also, people in leadership positions tend to favor their employees

who smile more regularly (though smiling too much in an interview, it was found, can make you seem less serious or competent).

4) **Smiling Improves Your Mood**—Smiling can put you in a good mood. It's been found that making yourself smile—*even when you're feeling down*—helps improve your mood and increases positive thoughts.

5) **Smiling Helps Lower Blood Pressure**—Smiling, combined with laughter, causes an initial increase in heart rate, followed by a period of muscle relaxation and a decrease in heart rate and blood pressure.

6) **Smiling Helps Relieve Stress**—Frustrated? Stressed? Smiling can result in a lower heart rate during these types of tasks. While stress typically increases your heart rate and blood pressure, smiling provides you with both psychological and physical health benefits.

7) **Smiling Improves Your Immune Function**—Laughter, beginning with a smile, appears to help boost your body's immune system. The laughter and positive thoughts release signaling molecules in your brain that fight stress and illness.

8) **Smiling Relieves Pain**—Laughter causes your body to release its own natural painkillers. Social laughter increases your pain threshold, creating a higher pain tolerance.

The moral of the story is to release those feel-good neurotransmitters—dopamine, endorphins, and serotonin—by smiling. You and all those around you will be glad you did.

A word of caution, though, to those of you who travel internationally, specifically on different hemispheres of the world. Did you know that most of this information comes from the western side of the world and as such, that makes these societies WEIRD? According to the study titled "Be Careful Where You Smile: Culture Shapes Judgements of Intelligence and Honesty of Smiling Individuals" by Kuba Krys et al., the authors reference WEIRD— *Western, Educated, Industrialized, Rich, Democratic*—societies as those where smiling individuals are judged as happier, more attractive, competent, and friendly.

While they don't dispute the benefits the other studies reference, they do point out a number of relevant points as it pertains to where you are in the world. Consider some of their findings. There is an old Russian proverb that states, "Smiling with no reason is a sign of stupidity." Similarly, a guidebook about Poland warns tourists that smiling at strangers is perceived by Poles as a sign of stupidity. The Norwegian government explains that when a stranger on the street smiles at locals, they may assume the stranger is insane.

Why the dichotomy? Different experiences and cultures will translate to different interpretations but the bottom line is this. When acted upon with genuineness and sincerity, your smile is a prelude to your superpowers of giving and gratitude.

I don't think the fact can be overstated in that when you "arm" yourself with your smile, you have the ability to alter and improve the lives around you. You have the power to enhance your own life on so many levels—your health, your mood, your relationships, your career—to rename a few. This simple but beautiful act is your gift to those you come across every single time, every single day. It's also the gift that you can keep giving not only to others, but to yourself.

***

What about gratitude? "How can smiling translate into gratitude?" you may be asking. I'm going to ask you to try an experiment I've been working on for the past few years. It involves the simple task of doing the following when you first wake up in the morning: Smile and say, *"Thank you, God, for this day."*

This practice instantly translates into a warm, happy feeling internally and proves to be a great start to my day.

Every day you wake up is a reason to give thanks, to express gratitude, to smile. They go hand-in-hand. A question may arise, though. Do you smile because you have things to be grateful for, or are you grateful because of the things you can smile about?

The answer to that question quite simply is, "Yes!"

However you phrase it, whichever way you choose to look at it, smiling and gratitude are like milk and cookies, peanut butter and jelly, or in my world, pretzels and ice cream (don't knock it until you try it, it's delicious). They complement each other because it's next to impossible to have one without the other.

Do a little experiment for me. We'll call it our latest "Things To Accomplish."

## TTA #4—You Can't Help but Smile

Go back to chapter 2 and look over your daily list titled "Thank You, God, for These Gifts in My Life." Read Day 1 out loud. You can read it to yourself but I find it more impactful when you read it aloud. Pause for a moment to really think about these things. Now, notice your reaction. If you are not grinning from ear to ear outwardly, I imagine they've brought you great joy internally.

Now, repeat these steps for the successive days. Do you feel "lighter?" It's as if burdens have been lifted, your shoulders are not so weighted down, your jaw isn't clenched so tightly, and ultimately, you feel like a new person, don't you? All of a sudden, your cares and concerns, while legitimate, have less power over you and your actions. Then behold. Your big, beautiful smile has once again returned. The lights in Times Square have nothing on that 10-million-watt smile of yours and you can't get over how great you feel.

This is the power of gratitude. This is the experience you'll have every time you take the time to truly get into a moment and reflect.

Another way that a smile can really impact you is when it comes from observation, when you watch it unfold from afar. It's when an experience occurs right in front of you but it's as if you're not even in the room. You might as well be invisible but wind up having a front-row seat.

That scenario happened to me at a Jersey Mike's. I was sitting at a table doing some work and a gentleman walked in. It was pouring down rain and he had stepped in to get dry. Despite being wet, however, he was very excited and announced that he was looking to confirm that the bus ran from just down the road of the restaurant. The reason? As he went on to tell those inside, *"I have my first job interview in years and I don't want to be late."* He went on to say, *"This is such a wonderful day and I'm so thankful."*

And, "Bam!" The excitement, sincerity, and appreciation in his voice were enough to make everybody within my view flash a grin. It was the type of smile that said, "Atta boy! You've got this! Go get 'em!" An employee confirmed that there was a bus that stopped there but that he wasn't sure of the time it ran. The employee also responded with a *"Sure,"* to the gentleman's request to sit in the restaurant for a few minutes to get dry.

That was all he needed to continue on his merry way but it wasn't enough for two women who were in line waiting to place their order. They called him over and offered to buy him a meal. You see, while he was certainly presentable in his appearance, they were able to tell that he needed a little bit more. After some back and forth jousting of *"Thanks, but that's not necessary"* and *"Oh, it's no problem,"* he relented and graciously accepted the meal. He then went on to tell those ladies—and despite his attempt to do so quietly, he had one of those amazing voices that doesn't know how to be turned down—he had earlier in his life served in the military and had run into some difficult times since being home.

He was so thankful for the dry space, the meal, and the kindness shown, he began to both beam with a beautiful smile, while simultaneously having tears stream down his face. He was so thankful, so grateful for the kindness of all those involved, he went on to ask God for His blessing for all the people who had helped him during this time and seemingly floated out the door and down to the bus stop.

What experience have you had that brings a smile to your face? Was it a random encounter like I had? Does it revolve around your wedding day? A pleasant childhood memory? A memory that makes you beam with pride surrounding your own children? Perhaps you were a poor student in school but there was this one time when you really studied hard and aced an exam? Or that day when after a lot of long hours and hard work, you finally received that promotion? Did you help somebody through a conversation, or by working with them to help him/her succeed? Whatever it was, take time to recall those events in your life.

Whatever the experiences, I'd like for you to write them down below. You may choose to write all the details of the event or simply the event itself. Either way, write out your top-five "Smile-Worthy Events." Can't rank some without including the others? Then make it your top seven or top ten. I'll leave some extra room at the bottom.

Following their listing, pause for a few moments to reflect and really appreciate the pride you have for these events. For **TTA #5**, we'll call them:

## <u>My Top-Five Smile-Worthy Events</u>

1. _____

   _____

2. _____

   _____

3. _____

   _____

4. _____

   _____

5. _____

   _____

# Chapter Eight
# Be Your Own Kind of Beautiful

*Stay True to Yourself and Listen to Your Inner Voice.*
*It Will Lead You to Your Dreams!*
—James Clark Ross

Throughout my years of reading books like this one, I love the fact that they pointed out suggestions that if incorporated in my life, would have a positive impact for a long time to come. And throughout your reading of this book, it is my sincere hope that you will come to a similar conclusion.

Here's the thing, though. For me or anybody to write or verbally say to you that *"this"* is the one and only way to accomplish what you wish for your life, would be doing a disservice. So let me be abundantly clear. I am not telling you that the only way to be, as James Clark Ross said above, "led to your dreams," is if you do everything exactly the way it is laid out with 100 percent accuracy.

The preceding is an outline that can indeed help you, however, and this is key: you must be true to you. You must utilize your life's experiences when you practice giving and gratitude in the ways that work best for you. Don't practice anything in a certain way because somebody told you to. Practice it in a way that feels right to you. The way that makes you happy and proud to be you. The way that makes your soul sing and has you in harmony with it.

Think about the fact that if the more successful people in life, however you define success, did things exactly the way somebody else told them to. Do you think they'd be as successful? Do you think their genuineness that has been discussed in this book would shine through if they did everything exactly the way somebody else did? Of course not. Successful lives that have been lived have been done through sincerity with regard to who those people truly are.

Let me give you an example.

For those of you who've played Little League Baseball, softball, or any other sport, think about your coach. He or she typically had some knowledge about the game and the desire to help kids get better at it. That said, when I was growing up, coaches would tell me, and every other kid, to hit a certain way. *"Bend your knees!"* and *"Elbow up!"* were a couple of the constant pieces of advice they'd give you. (For those of you with children who play baseball or softball, I'm sure you still hear the same time-honored coaching refrains today.) While their advice wasn't bad, and came from a good place, what it often led to was the kids being so conscious of doing things a certain way, that they became paralyzed by constantly thinking about how to hit and sometimes would not even swing because of this mental paralysis. If they did swing, they oftentimes looked very awkward, stiff, and robotic.

However, when hitters learned to bend their knees and keep their elbows up, combined with other tips, most importantly, standing in the batter's box in a way that was comfortable for them, they were generally more successful. Can you imagine watching a Major League Baseball game in which every hitter hit the exact same way? That would be terrible, not to mention the fact that we would not have the game we have today. If we had a game at all, it would be one filled with people trying to copy everybody else and not being true to who they were as a hitter (this applies to pitchers and fielders as well).

The same thing applies to living a life filled with giving and gratitude. While what has been laid out in this book is sound and, if followed, will make a difference in your life and the way you live it, let's remember for you to be you. You're the only one that can pull this off, this change, this transformation. But it has to be in such a way that it can't be mistaken for anybody else. It has to be uniquely you.

Speaking of Major League Baseball, do you know who Jeremy Jeffress is? Enjoying a solid career that began back in

2010, he was having his best season on the mound in 2018. During the season, his professional stock rose as a relief pitcher for the Milwaukee Brewers. More importantly, though, his personal stock rose as well.

One night at Miller Park—home of the Brewers—he was visiting a group of fans prior to the game. As he visited, he noticed a little boy crying away from the group he was visiting. He went on to learn that the little boy, Owen, all of four years old, forgot to bring his glove to the field. Upon learning the story, Jeffress let the boy have his glove for the game.

Before I tell you more of this story, let me explain something to you. I started playing baseball when I was three years old and was fortunate enough to play up to college baseball. Because of these experiences, I can tell you that ballplayers are a funny, quirky, and really superstitious bunch. There are some who have to put their uniform on a certain way every game. If you put the wrong sock on first, or button your jersey bottom-to-top instead of top-to-bottom, for example, you might as well tell the manager not to put you in today because you "know" you're going to have a bad game. There are at-bat rituals, things we have to draw out in the field with our spikes, pre-pitch moves and, a-hem, "adjustments" to make … and I can go on and on.

But I haven't even touched on how you never, ever, mess with another player's bats or dare try on a player's batting gloves. Worst of all, NEVER mess with his glove. I mean the act of another player putting his sweaty, dirty hand in your glove … quite possibly messing up the shape of it in those five seconds, though it took you months to get it just right … oh no, you NEVER do that! I mean, the way some guys feel about it, you might as well start breaking in a new glove because this one has been ruined.

Now understanding all of that, here comes this Major League pitcher, a player who more than likely has played his whole life, who just gives a four-year-old boy—who probably has sticky, grimy hands—his glove for the day. Impressive!

This, however, is where the story gets really interesting because according to David Gasper, who wrote the story for ReviewingTheBrew.com, a website through the company, FanSided, Owen's young sister, Bri, mom, and grandparents also were impacted. In fact, the grandfather, Robert Pollyea, wanted to repay the act of kindness so not only did he write a letter to the Brewers manager and front office explaining what had happened, but he also sent one to Dave Roberts, manager for the National League All-Star team. Roberts would go on to choose some of the players for the 2018 squad. Pollyea was hoping this letter would impact Roberts's decision.

Pollyea would go on to say, "This is not about me. It's about the player. He's a caring person with a franchise that seems to care about its fans. These are the types of stories that need to be told. I tried to represent him as a person." Though it is unclear whether his letter played into the decision, Jeffress was chosen as an All-Star replacement for another player who was injured. He went on to pitch a scoreless inning in the game.

But wait, the story goes on.

Weeks later, a box was delivered to Pollyea's home. Inside the package was an autographed Jeremy Jeffress jersey (say that five times fast) sent by the player upon learning of Pollyea's efforts to have him chosen as an All-Star. "He was so excited to tell me," said his wife, Dr. Sheri Doniger, who was on the phone with her husband when the package arrived.

Another example of a victorious cycle! In this case, I also believe Jeffress was being true to himself. Without ever having the pleasure to meet either the player or the man that he is, I say this because he acted on impulse. He didn't calculate in his mind, "Well, if I give him my glove, then these people are going to love me. And if they love me, they might go on and get me voted into the All-Star Game, and if that happens …" I don't for a second believe that any of that happened. It was purely instinct and it is a great example of being true to yourself.

The exciting thing is that there are so many stories like this. While they don't get told as often, it is so important to realize how prevalent they are in our society. Just because we sometimes have to look a little harder for them, doesn't mean they're not there. It certainly, for any reason, should never stop us from creating our own stories like this. We have the opportunity to positively impact another's life every single day of our life. Stories like Jeffress's remind me of that fact, as I hope it does for you as well.

It can be so difficult to find exemplary occurrences like this one. If you need help finding some of the good stories that are out there, I invite you to visit www.GoodNewsNetwork.org. It is filled with stories from around the globe that focus on the positive events that occur in the world.

\*\*\*

*Always be yourself, express yourself, have faith in yourself, do not go out and look for a successful personality and duplicate it.*
—Bruce Lee

I love this quote by the legendary Bruce Lee because it gets to the heart of what it means to be true to yourself. If enacted upon, it allows you to be confident in who you are because you ooze honesty, sincerity, confidence, and authenticity.

I'd like to break down that quote.

*"Be yourself."* While that's pretty straightforward and self-explanatory, I think it can be a lot more difficult depending on the situation you're in. Think about when you are around other people. It can be difficult to truly be yourself because not everybody—even if like-minded—is going to think and act exactly as you would. It can be a challenge but just because you may go along with a conversation doesn't mean you have to totally agree. Always remember to follow that inner thought or feeling, your soul, that will guide you.

*"Express yourself."* This too can be a challenge but remember if you're asked your opinion on a given topic, it's OK to have a different thought process and express that to others. There's always a trick to it and that trick is to not come across like your way is "right" and theirs is "wrong." Rather to express it in a matter-of-fact way that lets people know where you stand but not that your way is any better for them … just for you.

Another way of saying be confident in yourself is to say *"have faith in yourself."* In case you haven't figured it out yet, we don't always get what we want right away. It takes patience, persistence, and a deep, impassioned thought process that doesn't say you *can* do it but you *will* do it! There may be obstacles in your way, roadblocks put up, but don't ever lose faith in you.

I especially love the last part, *"do not go out and look for a successful personality and duplicate it."* That practically screams,

## "BE YOU!!!"

When you are indeed "you," the gift you are giving to the world is immeasurable. When you share your thoughts, dreams, and ideas with those you interact with, it inspires people. Not because all your thoughts, dreams, and ideas will always be in line with their thinking, but because it gives others the confidence to share theirs as well. You accomplish this through the passion you exude, the gleam in your eyes, and the sincerity in which you present yourself.

You don't have to get up on a stage and talk to tens, hundreds, or thousands of people. You don't have to record it on a CD, write a newsletter, or start your own podcast to explain who you really are. When you are true to yourself in your daily life and in the way you come across to others, in the confidence you have in yourself, and the way you present who you really are, it is truly an inspiration.

There are those who are great at this. They are already confident and have no problem letting the world know their beliefs. If you're not that type, don't worry about it. It's really irrelevant if others agree because the takeaway here is that you've shared a piece of you. You've enlightened others by sharing part of your innermost thinking … you've shared your soul. And that, my friends, is being authentic to who you really are.

\*\*\*

I'd like to discuss one last point. It revolves around a suggestion more than anything else. It can be very scary to some people but I ask you to consider this an important part of making any changes you decide to make upon the completion of this book. Don't worry, though, nobody has to know about it but you. It can be our little secret.

If you want to be successful at anything you do in life, there has to be some sort of accountability. It's important to know that nobody will be checking up on you. I'm not going to track every person who purchases this book and do a follow-up because the only one you have to be accountable to is you.

As I've referenced earlier, if you are looking to adapt your current thoughts and actions to ones more centered on giving and gratitude … and make them a lasting part of your life … you'll want to make sure there is a way to stay the course. In other words, don't do what I've done in the past when I get myself psyched up to, say, eat with a healthier lifestyle in mind. I start out great, eating a lot of crunchy foods like apples and carrots, as opposed to pretzels and chips. Come about midafternoon of Day 2 or so, I reason that "a few more won't hurt." Of course, a few becomes a lot the next day and all of a sudden, I'm back to thinking, "Maybe I'll *really* start next week."

I've got one more TTA for you to help avoid a similar outcome. You don't have to put your list in a place where everybody can see it. Just put it where only you can see it. Every day. Accountability in this case doesn't mean a weekly report that has to be done. No spreadsheets. No formulas to calculate. There is no phone call that has to be made to anybody reporting your progress.

### TTA #6—Oh, What a Week!

At the end of the week, simply write out some of the actions you've taken regarding ways you've given and ways you've expressed gratitude. I'm making room for five events but hope you will find yourself adding to that list. This will accomplish a couple of things:

1. It allows you to recognize some of the great things you've accomplished; AND
2. To see something written out allows you to build momentum going into the next week and subtly inspire you to continue on this trek.

# GIVING & GRATITUDE—
## WEEKLY REVIEW

1. _____

_____

2. _____

_____

3. _____

_____

4. _____

_____

5. _____

_____

6. _____

_____

7. _____

_____

In the beginning of this book, I told you that I like to tackle big obstacles as evidenced by sharing what I feel is the meaning of life. That is, of course, giving and gratitude. As you take this guideline toward achieving life's meaning, please remember to always to be true to yourself. When you get right down to it, as you search your soul, you will quickly come to realize that all the answers already lie within you.

My friends, I wish you much joy and success in your life. My wish is that all your dreams, whatever they may be, exceed even your own wildest expectations in your life.

May God continue to bless and help guide you along the way toward a life filled with giving and gratitude!

# Epilogue

Wow! What a journey this has been! Having been rejected by multiple agents, I finally found one. However, with no publisher initially interested, the agent and I unfortunately parted ways. Having practically given up on this book-writing experience, I wrote the fine people at Ozark Mountain Publishing, who saw the potential in what you have just read. Thank you, Nancy Vernon, Brandy McDonald, and all the wonderful people within Ozark for this opportunity. Thanks for the incredible efforts of my editor, Debbie Upton, who put the finishing touches on this book while putting up with my many, many questions.

It is truly my hope and dream that the information contained in this book will serve you well and help you to make lasting and impactful changes in the way you think about life as a whole.

In an effort to help provide a more direct path toward giving and gratitude, please find the following pages to be additional worksheets for the TTAs outlined in this book. Also, please review the websites from chapter 6 that will tell you more about the amazing companies referenced.

Lastly, I would be honored to hear from you. I'd love to learn your thoughts about what you have just read. Please contact me directly at CreatingOurReality@gmail.com. If I can help you, your company, or nonprofit organization in any way, please visit my website at www.CreatingOurReality.com.

Thank you.

# Additional Things To Accomplish
# Worksheets

## <u>TTA #1—Commitment of Three</u>

### Day 1

_____

_____

_____

_____

### Day 2

_____

_____

_____

_____

### Day 3

_____

_____

_____

_____

# TTA #2—Expressing Gratitude Regarding My Health

1. _____
   _____
   _____

2. _____
   _____
   _____

3. _____
   _____
   _____

## TTA #3—Thank You, God, for These Gifts in My Life

1. _____

2. _____

3. _____

4. _____

5. _____

1. _____

2. _____

3. _____

4. _____

5. _____

1. _____

2. _____

3. _____

4. _____

5. _____


1. _____

2. _____

3. _____

4. _____

5. _____


1. _____

2. _____

3. _____

4. _____

5. _____

# TTA #4—You Can't Help but Smile

Read out loud your list from TTA #2

## TTA #5—My Top-Five Smile-Worthy Events

1. _____

_____

2. _____

_____

3. _____

_____

4. _____

_____

5. _____

_____

# TTA #6—G&G Weekly Review

1. _____

_____

2. _____

_____

3. _____

_____

4. _____

_____

5. _____

_____

6. _____

_____

7. _____

_____

# About the Author

\* Keynote Speaker  \* Trainer \* Business Consultant

Known as "The SMART Guy" – Success Means Acquiring Right Thoughts – Anthony DeNino is the Founder and President of CORe – Creating Our Reality, Inc. Working with both For-Profit companies and Non-Profit organizations, his talks and training/workshops are targeted, interactive presentations, that are *customized* to fit the specific needs of the client. Utilizing his 25-years' experience in Corporate America, Anthony also consults with different companies and orginzations.

Among his areas of expertise include:

\* Motivation/Inspiration \* Leadership \*  Customer Service
\* Perspective \* Workplace Environment \* Sales
\* Effective Communication

CORe – Creating Our Reality, Inc.   704-236-8352   Charlotte, NC
www.CreatingOurReality.com

Follow him:

 @adenino

 Facebook.com/CreatingOurReality/

 Instagram.com/anthonydenino4/

# If you liked this book, you might also like:

*The Master of Everything*
by James Nussbaumer
*Mastering Your Own Spiritual Freedom*
by James Nussbaumer
*And Then I Knew My Abundance*
by James Nussbaumer
*Waking Up In The Spiritual Age*
by Dan Bird
*Finding Your Way In The Spiritual Age*
by Dan Bird
*Heaven Here on Earth*
by Curt Melliger
*Living the Life-Force*
by Nicholas Vesey

For more information about any of the above titles, soon to be released titles,
or other items in our catalog, write, phone or visit our website:
Ozark Mountain Publishing, Inc.
PO Box 754, Huntsville, AR 72740
479-738-2348
www.ozarkmt.com

For more information about any of the titles published by Ozark Mountain Publishing, Inc., soon to be released titles, or other items in our catalog, write, phone or visit our website:

Ozark Mountain Publishing, Inc.

PO Box 754

Huntsville, AR 72740

479-738-2348/800-935-0045

www.ozarkmt.com

# Other Books by Ozark Mountain Publishing, Inc.

**Dolores Cannon**
A Soul Remembers Hiroshima
Between Death and Life
Conversations with Nostradamus,
    Volume I, II, III
The Convoluted Universe -Book One,
    Two, Three, Four, Five
The Custodians
Five Lives Remembered
Jesus and the Essenes
Keepers of the Garden
Legacy from the Stars
The Legend of Starcrash
The Search for Hidden Sacred Knowledge
They Walked with Jesus
The Three Waves of Volunteers and the
    New Earth
**Aron Abrahamsen**
Holiday in Heaven
Out of the Archives – Earth Changes
**James Adams**
Little Steps
**Justine Alessi & M. E. McMillan**
Rebirth of the Oracle
**Kathryn/Patrick Andries**
Naked in Public
**Kathryn Andries**
The Big Desire
Dream Doctor
Soul Choices: Six Paths to Find Your Life
    Purpose
Soul Choices: Six Paths to Fulfilling
    Relationships
**Patrick Andries**
Owners Manual for the Mind
**Cat Baldwin**
Divine Gifts of Healing
**Dan Bird**
Finding Your Way in the Spiritual Age
Waking Up in the Spiritual Age
**Julia Cannon**
Soul Speak – The Language of Your Body
**Ronald Chapman**
Seeing True
**Albert Cheung**
The Emperor's Stargate
**Jack Churchward**
Lifting the Veil on the Lost Continent of
    Mu
The Stone Tablets of Mu

**Sherri Cortland**
Guide Group Fridays
Raising Our Vibrations for the New Age
Spiritual Tool Box
Windows of Opportunity
**Patrick De Haan**
The Alien Handbook
**Paulinne Delcour-Min**
Holy Ice
Spiritual Gold
**Anthony DeNino**
The Power of Giving & Gratitude
**Michael Dennis**
Morning Coffee with God
God's Many Mansions
**Carolyn Greer Daly**
Opening to Fullness of Spirit
**Anita Holmes**
Twidders
**Aaron Hoopes**
Reconnecting to the Earth
**Victoria Hunt**
Kiss the Wind
**Patricia Irvine**
In Light and In Shade
**Kevin Killen**
Ghosts and Me
**Diane Lewis**
From Psychic to Soul
**Donna Lynn**
From Fear to Love
**Maureen McGill**
Baby It's You
**Maureen McGill & Nola Davis**
Live from the Other Side
**Curt Melliger**
Heaven Here on Earth
**Henry Michaelson**
And Jesus Said – A Conversation
**Dennis Milner**
Kosmos
**Andy Myers**
Not Your Average Angel Book
**Guy Needler**
Avoiding Karma
Beyond the Source – Book 1, Book 2
The Anne Dialogues
The Curators
The History of God
The Origin Speaks

For more information about any of the above titles, soon to be released titles,
or other items in our catalog, write, phone or visit our website:
PO Box 754, Huntsville, AR 72740
479-738-2348/800-935-0045
www.ozarkmt.com

# Other Books by Ozark Mountain Publishing, Inc.

**James Nussbaumer**
And Then I Knew My Abundance
The Master of Everything
Mastering Your Own Spiritual Freedom
**Sherry O'Brian**
Peaks and Valleys
**Riet Okken**
The Liberating Power of Emotions
**Gabrielle Orr**
Akashic Records: One True Love
Let Miracles Happen
**Victor Parachin**
Sit a Bit
**Nikki Pattillo**
A Spiritual Evolution
Children of the Stars
**Rev. Grant H. Pealer**
A Funny Thing Happened on the
    Way to Heaven
Worlds Beyond Death
**Victoria Pendragon**
Born Healers
Feng Shui from the Inside, Out
Sleep Magic
The Sleeping Phoenix
**Michael Perlin**
Fantastic Adventures in Metaphysics
**Walter Pullen**
Evolution of the Spirit
**Debra Rayburn**
Let's Get Natural with Herbs
**Charmian Redwood**
A New Earth Rising
Coming Home to Lemuria
**David Rivinus**
Always Dreaming
**Richard Rowe**
Imagining the Unimaginable
**M. Don Schorn**
Elder Gods of Antiquity
Legacy of the Elder Gods
Gardens of the Elder Gods
Reincarnation...Stepping Stones of Life
**Garnet Schulhauser**
Dance of Eternal Rapture
Dance of Heavenly Bliss
Dancing Forever with Spirit

Dancing on a Stamp
**Manuella Stoerzer**
Headless Chicken
**Annie Stillwater Gray**
Education of a Guardian Angel
The Dawn Book
Joys of a Guardian Angel
Work of a Guardian Angel
**Blair Styra**
Don't Change the Channel
Who Catharted
**Natalie Sudman**
Application of Impossible Things
**L.R. Sumpter**
Judy's Story
The Old is New
We Are the Creators
**Artur Tadevlsyan**
Croton
**Jim Thomas**
Tales from the Trance
**Jason & Jolene Tierney**
A Quest of Transcendence
**Nicholas Vesey**
Living the Life-Force
**Janie Wells**
Embracing the Human Journey
Payment for Passage
**Dennis Wheatley/ Maria Wheatley**
The Essential Dowsing Guide
**Maria Wheatley**
Druidic Soul Star Astrology
**Jacquelyn Wiersma**
The Zodiac Recipe
**Sherry Wilde**
The Forgotten Promise
**Lyn Willmoth**
A Small Book of Comfort
**Stuart Wilson & Joanna Prentis**
Atlantis and the New Consciousness
Beyond Limitations
The Essenes -Children of the Light
The Magdalene Version
Power of the Magdalene
**Robert Winterhalter**
The Healing Christ

For more information about any of the above titles, soon to be released titles,
or other items in our catalog, write, phone or visit our website:
PO Box 754, Huntsville, AR 72740
479-738-2348/800-935-0045
www.ozarkmt.com